LONDON'S LEA VALLEY
A CENTURY OF GROWING

LONDON'S LEA VALLEY
A CENTURY OF GROWING

RESEARCHED AND WRITTEN BY
JIM LEWIS

ON BEHALF OF THE
LEA VALLEY GROWERS' ASSOCIATION

LIBRI
PUBLISHING

Published in 2011 by Libri Publishing

ISBN: 978 1 907471 59 9

A CIP catalogue record for this book is available from
The British Library

Design by James Hunnisett

Printed in the UK by Halstan Printing

Libri Publishing
Brunel House
VolunteerWay
Faringdon
Oxfordshire
SN7 7YR

Tel:+44 (0)845 873 3837
www.libripublishing.co.uk

ACKNOWLEDGEMENTS

The author wishes to thank the following organisations, companies and societies for their encouragement, support and advice and for supplying many of the illustrations within this book:

Bishopsgate Institute, 230 Bishopsgate, London

Bruce Castle Museum, Tottenham, London

Glinwell Plc, Smallford Nurseries, St Albans, Hertfordshire

Cheshunt Library, Turners Hill, Cheshunt, Hertfordshire

Enfield Local History Unit, Enfield, Middlesex

Epping Forest Museum, Waltham Abbey, Essex

Guy & Wright Ltd., Much Hadham, Hertfordshire

John Lewis/Waitrose Archive, Stevenage, Hertfordshire

Lea Valley Growers' Association, Archive, Turners Hill, Cheshunt

Lowewood Museum, Hoddesdon, Hertfordshire

Newham Local History Library, Stratford, London

Potters Bar Historical Society, Potters Bar, Hertfordshire

Royal Gunpowder Mills archive, Waltham Abbey, Essex

The Rochford family archive, Cambridgeshire

The South family archive, London Colney, Hertfordshire

Valley Grown Nurseries, Nazeing, Essex

While many individuals have freely given their knowledge, some unknowingly, which has contributed greatly to the production of this book, I have also paid special tribute to certain people in the book's reference section.

I could not let the occasion pass without recording my sincere thanks to my wife Jenny for her superb editorial skills and outstanding patience. The author freely admits that this voluntary sacrifice on Jenny's part has comprehensively tested the cement that holds our wonderful marriage together.

FOREWORD

A Word from the Chairman

As I sit here reflecting back over the last hundred years there seem to be some striking similarities between the growers of the Lea Valley Growers' Association (LVGA) of yesteryear and the LVGA of today. We have to irrigate, heat the crop, harvest it and control a wide range of pests and diseases – no change there then. Today we have a range of beneficial insects that combat almost all of the modern glasshouse pests. Modern pesticides are pest specific and seldom used in some protected edible crops, with almost no detectable residue levels in the produce when and if they are used. Modern plant breeding has enabled us to grow plants with greater resistance to a wider range of plant viruses and diseases.

We harvest vastly more product than ever before from an acre of land with minimal impact on the environment, green energy is key, carbon foot printing is today's buzzword but should we not concentrate our efforts on our water foot print? Although it's not something we should contemplate we can grow under glass without heat but to grow without water is impossible.

CHPs or combined heat and power plants provide not only heat but CO_2 generating excess electricity that can be fed back into the national grid. Take that one stage further and couple that CHP with an anaerobic digester that uses food waste, now we are really talking green energy. To have the ability to reduce landfill and use a product that was intended for waste as a source of heating – now that's clever joined up thinking.

The route to market was a day's cart ride from London, which is not too dissimilar from the route today but certainly more challenging as we look at a more global picture. Food safety is key; the market is driven by the perfect product at a price that does not necessarily reflect the cost and attention to detail throughout the supply chain. Do people recognise and support food that is locally produced in preference to cheaper, inferior imports? I'd like to think so but I think I need further convincing that the majority are not constrained by price alone in what and where they buy.

We are dominated by the one-stop-shop that is the modern retailer or supermarket. They determine our ever-decreasing returns as they seek to expand at a rate that is unimaginable with pre-tax profits that exceed the gross product of some third world countries. The rise and rise of the supermarket has been to the detriment of the smaller shop owners with many unable to compete with the volumes sold through the retail chain.

Food security and supply will focus the mind on an ever increasing world population. How do we feed nine billion mouths by 2050? Will genetically modified food be the shortcut answer we turn to in order to address this need? I am sure there are some easy wins before we arrive at that logical conclusion. Food waste is key. If we could reduce this significantly we could go a long way to achieving our goal. The buy one get one free mentality does little to address not only the greed factor but also has the potential to compound the food that goes to waste significantly. The challenge of the last fifty years was to double production which we did with an increase of only 15 percent extra land use nationally. Future water and energy storage will be the determining factor as to how we cope with the ever-changing world weather patterns. The suggestion is that we will have the same annual rainfall in the northern hemisphere as now but wetter winters and drier hotter summers. This will mean that if we do not address the water storage shortfall issue our crops long term will suffer. Parts of the world may become uninhabitable over time as the earth heats up, the world population may well migrate towards the northern hemisphere, greater emphasis will be placed on northern Europe to feed not only Europe but possibly the world, a significant challenge when you consider that the UK is not self sufficient in many, if any, foods on an annual basis.

The growers of London's Lea Valley have over time been instrumental in securing not only food for London but for the wider UK markets. Historically we supplied both edible and ornamental produce to the wholesale market. At its peak in the 1960s the growers of the Lea Valley were responsible for the largest area of glass anywhere in the world. The crops supplied changed as did the nationality of the growers who supplied that produce. In the 1960's we saw a slow change of glasshouse use away from what was traditionally grown towards cucumber production with the arrival in the Lea Valley of the Sicilian growers. Further additions to the already diverse crops grown were evident towards the end of the 20th century with sweet peppers and aubergines replacing tomatoes and cucumbers.

One recurring theme since the early 1960s is the increased competition with our Dutch cousins as they seek to export around 90 percent of all agricultural and horticultural produce that is oversupplied to their home market. Prices in the UK have over time been influenced by the drive for Holland to export their produce at a price that is barely breakeven at times. The recent poor price of the pound against the euro has one benefit in that produce that would have come to the UK is going to other EU countries in preference to our own.

Over time the crop workers have also changed. We are part of the EU, with 27 member states with more waiting to join, citizens of many of those are able to work in the UK. Over the last 5–10 years we have seen an ever-increasing Polish workforce fill vacancies.

How will the glasshouses of the future look? I suspect the harvesting will all be done automatically, the plants will tell us what they require to grow to the optimum, greater feedback and interaction between them and the computer software will take some of the skill away from the grower, a fully automated glasshouse with no staff, difficult to imagine now but not impossible. How many times does science fiction become science fact?

In 1911 the LVGA was set up with the goal of representing growers on a political lobbying front. The emphasis changed over the years but today the LVGA is firmly representing our growers again at both local and national MP level but also encroaching into Brussels with regular contact with our MEPs for certain issues like the 91414 pesticide directive.

Both locally and on a national level we have seen some challenging times, none more so than the recent e-coli outbreak in Northern Germany. There comes a moment, a catalogue of circumstances that has the potential to decimate a whole section of protected edibles by a wrongful diagnosis of the source of the outbreak. The repercussions of this were felt throughout Europe with dire consequences to growers, marketing and retailers alike as consumer confidence dipped to the point where most of the protected edible crops were also targeted, as the real source of the outbreak was left in doubt. When lives are lost and (one life is one too many) it focuses the mind; if in doubt don't eat cucumbers, tomatoes, lettuce. They were all implicated at one point. Still not sure? Then I won't eat aubergines or peppers because there was a picture of one on the BBC website. From the original suggested source it became clear that were a number of crops affected either directly or by association. In living memory there has never been a food scare where lives have been lost from UK-grown produce. I know this is tempting fate but is a true reflection of the high regard given to food safety in the UK and by local growers.

To restore consumer confidence Epping Forest and local businesses have come together to celebrate the humble cucumber by way of a festival. The Great British National Cucumber Festival will celebrate not only cucumbers but all produce grown in the Lea Valley and connect with local businesses and interest groups. The main theme will be cucumbers either directly or by association; in Pimms drinks; in Victorian kitchen sandwiches; who can grow the largest cucumber? And a 4 x 100 cucumber relay to rival the Olympics of 2012. There will be various zones, a growing zone, little Italy, a children's zone and various local businesses and interest groups all coming together in celebration of the Lea Valley. More importantly we will donate the proceeds of the event which we hope will be an annual national event to a number of local children's charities.

As a specialist sector representing horticulture we are a resilient group that survives by our own dogged reluctance to give up. Unlike other sectors of industry we continue with little or no subsidy but continue we do. Bring on the next century; we have survived for the last hundred years and continued to grow despite these challenges. What the challenges are for the next century no one knows but I suspect they will be much the same as the last century. The emphasis may change but the principles remain the same; crops need irrigating, heating, harvesting and we will still need a route to market. All I do know is we need to be proactive, resilient and have the ability to see change as a positive but of this I am sure; survive and prosper we will.

Gary Taylor, Chairman LVGA, 2011

ABOUT THE AUTHOR

Dr. Jim Lewis has spent most of his career in the consumer electronics industry, apart from a three-year spell in the Royal Air Force servicing airborne and ground wireless communications equipment. When working in the Lea Valley for Thorn EMI Ferguson he represented the company abroad on several occasions and was involved in the exchange of manufacturing technology. Currently he is a Consultant to Terry Farrell & Partners on the historical development of London's Lea Valley and a Workers' Educational Association (WEA) tutor teaching industrial history. He also teaches students within the Community Programme who have learning difficulties. A freelance writer, researcher and broadcaster for his specialist subject – London's Lea Valley, he also has a genuine passion for encouraging partnership projects within the local community, which in the long term, are planned to help stimulate social and economic regeneration. Dr. Lewis is married with four grown-up children and lives in Lincolnshire.

The author Dr Jim Lewis with Isaac his youngest grandson

TWO LEA VALLEY GROWERS

Jim Lewis was commissioned to research and write this book by the Lea Valley Growers' Association. Two people in particular have been involved at all stages and the book would not have been published without their support and help.

Lee Stiles

Born in the Lea Valley and raised in the Epping Forest District, Lea Valley Growers' Association secretary Lee Stiles' childhood memories stir from stories told by his Grandmother and Aunt of when they were blown out of a Lea Valley Tomato glasshouse when they were sent to work there during the war. Lee took the position of secretary at the Lea Valley Growers' Association in 2008 after holding the position of National Farmers' Union Group secretary in West Essex looking after the interests of Arable and Livestock Farmers in the region.

Gary Taylor

Gary Taylor was born in 1959 in West Sussex, the eldest of three sons of Diana and Walter – Kevin and Peter being the younger sons. After leaving school he attended The West Sussex College of Agriculture and Horticulture where he spent the next five years. On leaving college he worked for the Van Heyningen Brothers (VHB) while continuing his horticulture development until he left in 1995 to work in Somerset for Thomas Jones of Cantelo Nurseries as company production manager. In 2000 he made the move to Valley Grown Nurseries (VGN) to take over what was then Langridge Nurseries in the heart of the Lea Valley a stone's throw from London. It was then he became involved with the local growers' association the LVGA. His current involvement is as chairman but he represents his sector on various boards and steering groups for the NFU, HDC and the Red Tractor Food Assurance scheme. He is also the founder and current chairman of The Pepper Technology Group.

AUTHOR'S NOTE

Writing this centenary book has not been without its research challenges as I tried to interpret the sometimes sketchy information contained within the early minute books of the Lea Valley Growers' Association. On many occasions I struggled to make rational judgements, sometimes reading between the lines, when attempting to make sense of the material. After a lifetime of working in industry, business and academia, mostly in the Lea Valley region I have been fortunate in being able to tap into a reservoir of practical experience and knowledge which has allowed me to make what I hope the reader will see as reasonable assessments and observations.

Within this book it will be noted that occasionally, particularly when I have made an observation regarding an action taken by those early growers, I have reflected on their pronouncements and then posed a question. This approach is deliberate to allow us all to consider that if faced with a similar set of circumstances as our ancestors, and now armed with the knowledge and experience of how today's markets and industry work, would we still choose to follow the same route or, in the light of acquired wisdom, do something radically different? This book has been written as I followed the minutes of the Lea Valley Growers' Association in an historical time-line. In following the progress of the Association and its members during the development of the region's horticultural industry the reader may detect that my views occasionally altered.

When information in the Association's early minute books was sparse I was forced to explore alternative sources. This has allowed me to see that several quite different industries in the Lea Valley region were interconnected and influenced each other and also how seemingly unrelated events can have a profound effect upon those industries.

Researching and writing this book, at a time of severe world economic problems, has allowed me to ponder an age-old problem which I have seen many businesses fail to address. When running what appears to be a successful business it is extremely important for the owners to examine systems regularly and to ask themselves whether they have the mechanisms in place to combat a sudden external change in the marketplace, such as a rise in material or commodity prices. As a good friend once said to me: "When you begin to believe that your business is most successful, that is when your business is most vulnerable".

When accepting the commission to write this book I was asked if I could write a history that would not only be of interest to the Lea Valley Growers' Association but would also accommodate the interests of a wider readership. This I have tried to achieve, but ultimately the reader will have to judge if I have succeeded in meeting this challenge.

Jim Lewis

CONTENTS

INTRODUCTION

Most people would probably believe that the Lea Valley region is famous only for its plethora of world changing industrial and scientific firsts, but that would be a false assumption. The truth is the Lea Valley has a long and proud association with both horticulture and agriculture and this has actively encouraged a range of supporting industries and service providers to develop and set up in the region.

Referring to the Domesday Book it can be seen that there was considerable farming and smallholding activity in the area as our distant ancestors began to learn the skills and techniques of planting and husbandry which helped to support and sustain a growing population.
It is hard to imagine that an area like today's Newham, with its rapidly changing skyline as the borough prepares to host the 2012 Olympics, was growing potatoes on a commercial scale from the early eighteenth century. To help with the harvesting of the crop, Irish labour had to be imported to lift and collect the tubers which were becoming an important part of the daily diet of people in Britain.

Green Street House, known as Boleyn Castle. West Ham FC took out a lease on the site in 1904.

West Ham United Football Club which now stands on the site of St. Edward's Reformatory School where around 200 boys received agricultural training.

Growing vegetables was fairly common in east London at the turn of the twentieth century and areas of cultivation seemed to crop up (pardon the pun) in the most unlikely places. During the nineteenth century, the fundamentals of agriculture were taught to the two hundred boys of St Edward's Roman Catholic Reformatory School on the fourteen acres of land attached to the school building – Green Street House, East Ham. This agricultural land has now become the present home of West Ham United Football Club.

Dr John Fothergill (1712–1780) who was acknowledged as creating one of the finest private gardens in Europe on his West Ham estate.

The Quaker, Dr John Fothergill (1712–1780) purchased Upton House in West Ham (now Newham) in 1762 and set up home and also his doctor's practice.

Here, in the grounds of his house (now West Ham Park) he established a botanical garden which, at the time, rivalled the Royal Botanical Gardens at Kew. Apart from growing exotic fruit and plants in hothouses that he had built, he planted shrubs and trees from around the world that could be used as a basis for new medicines and also food. Astonishingly his plant collection amounted to over 3,400 different species. Sir Joseph Banks, the eminent botanist who had sailed with Captain James Cook on his first voyage of discovery (1768–1771), was so impressed with Fothergill's work and ingenuity that he wrote:

At an expense seldom undertaken by an individual and with an ardour that was visible in the whole of his conduct, he procured from all parts of the world a great number of the rarest plants, and protected them in the amplest buildings which this or any other country has seen.

In the 1740s, Johann Busch (anglicised to John Busch or John Bush) arrived in Hackney from Germany and became a supplier of unusual plants to several botanical gardens and in particular to those of Princess Augusta, daughter-in-law of George II. Augusta's plant collection was to eventually form the basis for the Royal Botanic

Gardens at Kew. Busch's work appears to have got him noticed and he was invited to Russia by Catherine the Great and commissioned to lay out gardens in the 'English-style'.

Not long after Busch, in the early 1760s, another German Joachim Conrad Loddiges, a gardener, settled in Hackney. After working to landscape the grounds of Dr (later Sir) John Baptist Silvester he set up in business as an importer of rare seeds and plants. Many of these he cultivated in large steam heated hothouses that he had built on a site in Mare Street, Hackney approximately where the Town Hall stands today. When hardy, many of these plants were exported overseas in special packaging which Loddiges had designed.

Joachim Conrad Loddiges (1738–1826). In the late 18th century Loddiges founded a nursery in Hackney.

The Botanical Gardens, Madeira, one of the many places supplied by Loddiges of Hackney with tea plants.

In the early nineteenth century, plants from the Loddiges Nursery were sent to Madeira where they helped to establish a successful tea plantation on the island. As the popularity of the Loddiges Nursery grew, plants were supplied to the royal parks and also to the great estates of Woburn Abbey and Chatsworth. When

the building used for the Great Exhibition of 1851 was relocated (in 1854) from Hyde Park to the site at Crystal Palace, Sydenham, a massive Mauritius fan palm weighing around fifteen tons left the Loddiges Nursery to adorn the building, making its way by road to its new destination pulled by thirty-two horses.

As the nineteenth century progressed the march of industry continued, fuelled by the expansion of the railways, and pressure across East London mounted for sites to build new factories and also houses for the rapidly growing population that had been attracted to the area by the promise of work. This made smallholding and nursery land an obvious target for the developers and as the factories took hold in the lower Lea Valley their presence caused increased levels of atmospheric pollution and also severe poisoning of water courses. As might be imagined this made the area less favourable to growers and it became a case of either closing down or moving out. The attraction of cheaper land in the cleaner environment of the upper Lea Valley made districts like Enfield, Waltham Cross, Waltham Abbey, Cheshunt and Nazeing ideal places for established and new growers to put down their roots. There was also the added attraction that the London markets were only a horse and cart journey away.

From the beginning of the nineteenth century a number of small nurseries had set up in the region of the upper Lea Valley. According to the late Peter Rooke, whose grandfather George had run nurseries in the Lea Valley, these were little more than open patches of ground where vegetables and bedding plants were grown out of doors. By the end of the century, with pressure on the lower Lea Valley growers to move due to the clamour of industry for building land, it had become clear that the upper Lea Valley offered the best opportunities for those who wished to start again.

As the upper Lea Valley growers had no doubt been drawn to this part of the region by its fertile loams and abundant water supplies, the area must have looked extremely attractive to those who were being forced out of areas of London polluted by industry, which had a long way to go before it came under legally enforceable environmental controls. With the lower region's growers moving into the area alongside their upper Lea Valley counterparts it would have probably seemed obvious to these early pioneers that as their numbers increased they could collectively become a dominant force in Britain's horticultural industry. However, for this to happen, the growers would need to come together as an organised group.

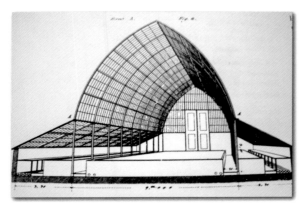

A drawing of Loddiges Grand Palm House where plants were supplied to decorate the Great Exhibition of 1851.

A Giant Mauritius fan palm pulled by 32 horses, on its way to the re-erected Crystal Palace at Sydenham, South London c.1854.

OFFICERS OF THE LEA VALLEY GROWERS' ASSOCIATION

Presidents

Mr H. O. Larsen	(1911–1934)
Mr J. P. Rochford	(1934 –1961)
Mr B Rochford	(1962–
Mr L R Leach	
Mr T Rochford	
Mr M R Dyke	(1980 –1995)
Mr R. N. Copping	(1995–Present)

Life Vice Presidents (1994 to Present)

J J Allison, H S Beard, C D Chapman, P C Chapman, A Dyke, A J Parker, A G Roberts, T C Rochford

Chairmen

Mr H O Larsen	(1911-1916)
Mr M Dudding	(1911-1916)
Mr C H Shoults	(1916-1919)
Mr J P Rochford	(1919 –
Mr R Minard	
Mr L C Madsen	
Mr L R Leach	
Mr J Ritsema	(1962-1965)
Mr B F Meering	(1965–
Mr P J Butterfield	
Mr H S Beard	(1976–1980)
Mr T C Rochford	(1980–1987)
Mr L A Dingemans	(1987–1994)
Mr J H Mason	(1994–2000)
Mr D J Everett	(2000–2004)
Mr J H Mason	(2004- 2005)
Mr G. C. Taylor	(2005–Present)

Secretaries

Mr J C Cobley (Hon)	(1911–1913)
Mr W Dudding	(1913 -1914)
Mr A B Lister	(1914–1928)
Mr F H Fullom	(1928–1946)
Mr H Drew	(1946–1975)
Mr R A Stevenson	(1975–2008)
Mr L Stiles	(2008–present)

THE FOUNDING FATHERS

On Tuesday 31st October 1911 a meeting of representatives from the Nurserymen and Growers of the Lea Valley was convened at the Imperial Club, Waltham Cross when a resolution was moved by the Chairman and passed by those attending: "That an Association be formed which shall be called 'The Lea Valley and District Nurserymen's and Growers' Association". The passing of a second resolution set the annual membership subscription at ten shillings and six pence (half-a-guinea) that would translate to 52.5 pence in today's money! Unfortunately the minutes of the meeting do not list all those in attendance so we are unable to compare the numbers of those initially taking up membership of the organisation with the current membership of The Lea Valley Growers' Association, as today's organisation has become known.

NOVEMBER 29, 1922.   THE HORTICULTURAL TRADE-JOURNAL.   35

Our Artist's Impressions of Some of the Growers at the Lea Valley Dinner.

An artist's impression of some prominent Lea Valley growers from The Horticultural Trade Journal November 29, 1922

It is clear from the minutes that the nurserymen and growers were facing a number of quite serious challenges which they had reasonably concluded would only stand a chance of being resolved if they came together as a bona fide organisation. By forming an Association the growers felt that they would have a better opportunity to solve their problems collectively as certain government agencies would only recognise those organisations that were properly constituted.

The minutes of the first meeting reflect a number of outstanding concerns that the growers wanted addressed and, during discussion, the following issues were raised:

(a)   The study of the various insect and fungoid pests and diseases which were yearly increasing.

(b)   The question of rating which had just been discussed at the meetings of the Cheshunt District Council.

(c)   Lectures.

(d)   Difficulties with the Railway Companies, Market Salesmen etc.

While later minutes show that not all the growers' problems could be resolved by coming together as an Association, they do demonstrate that the organisation rapidly grew in stature and was acting in a professional and democratic way on behalf of its members.

As early as January 1912 the organisation had been incorporated as a limited liability company and a programme of lectures had been arranged on subjects appropriate to the members' requests. Later that year correspondence had begun with the Great Eastern Railway (GER) over its inadequate provision of goods sidings at local stations and also that company's inability to accept manure at Enfield Lock Station. Also deals had been negotiated with insurers and a ten percent discount on premiums for employer's liability insurance had been secured for members with the Legal Insurance Company.

By November, after listening to advice from Dr Russell of the agricultural Rothamsted Experimental Station, Harpenden, a special sub-committee of growers was formed. Soon the sub-committee was recommending that members should seriously consider a highly ambitious scheme to set up a local experimental station to carry out scientific work for the organisation. Should the recommendation be approved, then costs for setting up and running the station would be shared partially by funds raised by the growers. The Association would also approach the Board of Agriculture and the County Councils of Essex, Hertfordshire and Middlesex for grants to make up the outstanding costs for the station's continued upkeep.

In the following year representation was made by the Council of the Association to the Board of Trade over the practice undertaken by some wholesalers and retailers of removing labels from tomatoes, cucumbers and grapes grown abroad so they could be passed off as English produce. Presumably this devious removal of labelling was done so that the perpetrators could command a higher price for their produce. While it would be naive to believe that the Council could win every battle taken up on behalf of its members, the minutes show that the Council representatives went about their duties with a great deal of dedication and energy. They were certainly not afraid to tackle the major service providers over cost increases and there was no hesitation in confronting government departments on issues such as tax and legislation that affected the horticultural industry. The Lea Valley and District Nurserymen's and Growers' Association had begun the task of supporting its members with great enthusiasm; getting this newly formed body off to a flying start.

OUR PORTRAIT GALLERY.

BRITISH GLASSHOUSE PRODUCE MARKETING ASSOCIATION, LIMITED.—MEMBERS OF COMMITTEE.

Top Row Left to Right—A. B. Lister (Sec.). A. R. Wills. J. C. Cobley. C. C. Chorley. C. F. Camburn. G. N. Edwick.
Front Row Left to Right.—C. H. Shoults. G. F. Shoults. J. Harnett (Vice-Chairman). E. S. Shoults (Chairman). C. J. Randall (Hon. Treasurer). A. A. Pollard. R. Minard.
Absent Members of the Committee.—N. G. Bonaparte-Wyse. A. J. Henriksen. S. Holmberg. A. G. Linfield. J. Poupart. E. Stevens.

Members of the British Glasshouse Produce Marketing Association Committee, July 1925

THE FIRST WORLD WAR

On 28th July 1914, a little over two years after the formation of the Association, Britain was plunged into war with Germany and the effects of the conflict, which was to last until 11th November 1918, would throw up a number of substantial new challenges for Lea Valley growers. Unfortunately the minutes of the Association are incomplete between February and September 1914 but we are given a clue about the shape of things to come from the October minutes when "A vote of thanks to Mr Dudding for his work as Secretary and best wishes for his success and safe return in military service" was proposed.

It was not just the national call to arms that was appealing to the patriotic spirit of the men of the Lea Valley horticultural industry; it was also another call coming from much closer to home that was causing concern amongst the growers. The minutes of the growers' meeting of January 1915 record that Mr Larsen had been appointed to "...see Colonel Fisher on the subject of curtailing the amount of local labour attracted to the powder factories to the detriment of the nursery industry". One of these attractions was probably the better terms and conditions that manufacturing industries could offer the not so well paid workers employed in horticulture, a problem that would dog Lea Valley growers for years to come.

Colonel F T Fisher R A was superintendent at the Royal Gunpowder Mills, Waltham Abbey, an explosives factory that had been in government control since 1787.

Cordite press workers at the Royal Gunpowder Mills. The mills attracted workers away from the Lea Valley nursery industry during World War One.

During the First World War the mills were not only manufacturing gunpowder, they were also developing, producing and refining different types of explosives as well as certain chemicals. With pressure to increase the production of munitions coming from both government and the military, it is doubtful whether the Association would have had any influence when confronting Colonel Fisher regarding the movement of workers from horticulture to the gunpowder mills. However, it is clear that the Association had thought of other ways that the problem might be tackled.

At the October 1916 Annual General Meeting, the Secretary reported that through correspondence with various government departments they had been able to take "an active part in getting skilled workers in the fruit growing section of the nursery industry classed as members of a reserved occupation". This meant that should a worker receive his call-up papers for military

Clonel F T Fisher, Superintendent of the Royal Gunpowder Mills, Waltham Abbey (1909 - 1917)

A propaganda postcard to try and lift spirits on the home front.

Posters like this one encouraged Lea Valley nursery workers to volunteer

A poster inviting women to join the Women's Land Army during World War One.

service he could choose to remain with his employer. Now, through this recognition, certain members of the Lea Valley horticultural industry would be classed on a par with coal miners and other skilled workers whose jobs were seen as crucial to the war effort.

The labour problems concerning the growers would continue throughout the war as many of the industries in Britain had been taken over by government in an effort to increase production of munitions and other essential equipment for the allied forces and it was these manufacturers that were desperate for labour. This meant that horticultural workers who had not been granted reserved occupation status could either be conscripted into the armed forces if they were physically fit or, if they failed their medical, they might choose to work for one of these government-controlled industries which were probably perceived to have much stronger connections with the war effort than horticulture, not to mention the prospect of better pay.

As thousands of men in the U K had volunteered or had been conscripted to fight for their country, the jobs that they had vacated were taken over by women. The First World War is the first time in the history of Britain that women replaced skilled men in almost every workplace area (not just industry) and after a period of training were found to be equal to the work of men. While the minutes of the Association during the War years are not always regular, detailed or explanatory, particularly with regard to labour shortages and the

employment of women, there are one or two clues that can be extracted from these records where conclusions can be drawn. For example, an instruction is given to the Secretary at the Association's AGM of November 1914 that he should "write to the Belgian Refugee Committee and ask if they would be in a position to supply any horticultural labour for the spring time to local nurserymen". The Council minutes of May 1916 record that a grower reported that he has "received four summonses in respect of non-stamping of National Insurance Cards for temporary women workers". These brief references would indicate that there were serious labour shortages amongst the nurserymen and also that growers were wrestling with new forms of legislation that they had never before encountered, due to the employment of women.

In 1915 another wartime problem to beset the growers was the commencement of the world's first Blitz. This resulted in the deliberate targeting of the civilian population as the enemy tried to weaken morale and resolve, not just that of civilians but their relatives and loved ones fighting on the Western Front and elsewhere overseas. A great deal of the enemy action over Britain took place in the air space above the Lea Valley. This geographical region formed part of the London Air Defence Area (LADA). To deal with this new threat, several gun emplacements had been installed around the region and these were manned by gun crews from the Royal Artillery. These Anti Aircraft (AA) batteries had been put in place, along with searchlight batteries, to form a defensive shield around the capital to complement the work of the Royal Flying Corps who patrolled the sky above.

Two of the local gun emplacements, Monkhams Hall, Waltham Abbey and Pole Hill, Chingford, were part of the Northern sector of LADA, an area comprising some eighteen guns. Invading Zeppelins, on a mission to bomb London, often came under attack from these guns as the airships made their way south, losing height, so that their observers could identify designated targets in the capital. (It would be interesting to discover if there are any recorded incidents of growers encountering damage to their valuable glasshouses by the shock waves created by the guns as they blasted away at their leviathan targets.)

On the night of 2nd October 1916, one of Germany's new super airships, Zeppelin L31, commanded by the ace pilot Heinrich Mathy, was on a mission to bomb London. After making landfall at Lowestoft, Suffolk at approximately 8.00pm, he skirted the towns of Hertford and Ware as he made his way down country towards the Capital. North of Waltham Abbey Mathy came under intense fire from two separate anti-aircraft gun batteries; one of these was probably the one at Monkhams, positioned on the hill overlooking the Crooked Mile.

Zeppelin L31 responsible for destroying Lea Valley glasshouses.

To lighten the airship in an effort to gain height, Mathy released his complete bomb load in the hope of putting the Zeppelin beyond the range of the barrage from the ground. His descending missiles fell on Cheshunt, damaging over 340 houses and destroying some six and a half acres of glass which comprised all 40 glasshouses belonging to the Walnut Tree Nurseries.

Interestingly, the Association's 1911 minute book records a Mr J C Cobley residing at Walnut Tree House, Cheshunt. The minute book also shows that Mr Cobley was elected Honorary Secretary at the inaugural meeting, making him a member of the Association's Council. While the minutes of the Association for the First World War period are incomplete the minutes of the fifth AGM held on 20th October 1916 show a Mr G H Cobley being re-elected as Honorary Auditor. Also the minutes of the Association for the 15th December 1916 record a Mr R S Cobley being in attendance. As it is likely that both of the Cobleys were related to the Association's founder member, Mr J C Cobley, this might suggest that they were probably connected, or perhaps lived, at the Walnut Tree Nursery. Therefore, it is surprising that there is no mention in the minutes of the Zeppelin raid that had wiped out an entire collection of a member's glasshouses. Could it be that the recording of such incidents was thought to be unwise, or perhaps such details were banned by the authorities in case the information fell into the wrong hands?

At a General Meeting of the Association held in December 1916, the President, Mr H O Larsen explained that the meeting had been specifically called to discuss "potato culture under glass". This was in relation to a conference he had recently attended, presided over by the Chief Inspector of the Board of Agriculture. After much discussion by the members a resolution was passed, with three abstentions, agreeing to dedicate an area of glass amounting to about five percent of the growing area of those nurseries with suitable soil for the cultivation of potatoes. This action would seem to suggest that the wartime sinking of merchant shipping by the German High Seas Fleet was beginning to have a serious effect on Britain's supplies which was no doubt being felt by the civilian population with the absence of food in the shops.

Reading the minutes of the May meeting of the Association in 1917 further evidence of food shortages can be deduced when it was reported that a number of members had received notices from the government requiring them to "plough up all land laid down to grass since 1872 and sow the same with corn for the harvest of 1918". The advice given by the Association to those who had been contacted was to return the form stating "the impracticability of growing a successful crop of corn, or offering his land to the government according to the individual circumstances". The attempt by government to get the Lea Valley growers to convert their land to cereal production coincided almost directly with the increased German U-Boat attacks on merchant shipping bringing supplies to Britain which had begun in earnest by March 1917. Many of these attacks were against American and Canadian supply ships as they crossed the North Atlantic and this action would eventually draw the Americans into the war in Europe.

The food shortages caused by the increased torpedoing of merchant shipping encouraged the British government to impose a system of rationing to help create a fairer distribution of staple foods across the population. It was also an effort to try and alleviate malnutrition that had been on the increase amongst some of the country's poorest working-class families. Sugar was the first foodstuff to be rationed in January 1918 followed by other commodities such as meat, butter, margarine, cooking fat and cheese. The population was issued with ration cards which had detachable coupons allowing for a weekly quantity of 15 ounces of meat, 4 ounces of fats and 5 ounces of bacon. Ration card holders had to register with a butcher and a grocer. While the weekly quantities might appear harsh it was a fairer way of food distribution as their introduction, along with price controls, made hoarding almost impossible and also helped to reduce the number of people queuing outside the grocers and butchers who were now allocated controlled amounts of stock.

Food was not the only commodity rationed during the war. Coal, a necessary fuel for heating the glasshouses of the horticultural industry and for generating the electricity that powered the factories that produced munitions and other essential goods while providing the motive power for much of the shipping and the railways, had been strictly limited for domestic use by wartime regulation. Premises with three to five rooms were allowed a weekly supply of 2 cwt, those with six to seven rooms 4 cwt, while those with over twelve rooms could have 8 cwt. It became an offence under the wartime regulations to waste cinders and notices were published in newspapers of how to make briquettes out of coal-dust, clay and tar to use as a fuel for cooking purposes. It would appear that the increasing shortages of food had pricked the conscience of Lea Valley growers and

this is reflected in the minutes of the January 1918 General Meeting, attended by sixty-six members. Guest speakers at the meeting were a Dr Keeble and Mr McKay who each spoke about the "possibilities of nurserymen increasing the food supply of the nation at the present time". Following the talk a resolution was passed that was carried unanimously to "devote 5% of their glasshouse area to the cultivation of lettuces and radishes". Some growers offered to "grow cauliflowers as well". While this initiative of the growers might not appear that significant to a twenty-first-century observer, it does show a collective responsibility on the part of the Association to support the nation at a time of crisis.

The various requests from government to the Lea Valley Growers' Association to increase or diversify crop production to help supplement the nation's falling food stocks, allows us an insight into how quickly the Association had become established as a professional and respected body in the eyes of those running the country. Further confirmation of this can be gained from the Council minutes of April 1918 when a letter from the Board of Agriculture was read asking the Association to "nominate a representative to serve on the proposed Horticultural Advisory Board". Joseph Rochford was proposed in his absence and the motion was carried unanimously. (Mr Rochford was contacted from the meeting by telephone and agreed to accept the position). These various approaches, made to the Association by government and other national bodies, give us a clear indication that the Lea Valley region had become an important and established part of Britain's food economy.

Parade outside Buckingham Palace to celebrate end of WW1 (1919)

AFTER THE WAR AND UP TO THE 1930S

The period directly after the war saw the beginning of a slow return to normality for Lea Valley growers with the establishment of a Demobilisation Committee to ease the release of the male horticultural workers from their wartime industrial employment back to their peacetime occupations. This inevitably meant that women, who had been taken on to work in horticulture and other essential areas in place of men, would have to return once again to domesticity. However, the skills they had obtained doing vital war work would change, albeit slowly, the future attitudes of employers to a woman's competence in the workplace.

The minutes of the Association directly after the cessation of hostilities seem typically British and do not record anything about the momentous international event that had just passed. There were rather mundane discussions at the Council meeting on 12th February 1919 with regard to the "minimum rates of pay for capable nursery workers" which seem to have petered out without a recommendation, the final solution being "that the matter be left for individual consideration". A further discussion took place "on the desirability of adopting a standard type motor lorry for nursery traffic" and on this occasion the decision was taken to refer this task to a "special Sub Committee to report to the Council on the matter". However, there was one interesting resolution submitted by the Co-op Working Sub Committee, which was unanimously accepted by the meeting that "steps be taken to form a registered Cooperative Trading Society among the Lea Valley Growers". This would suggest that the growers had recognised the desirability of forming a body that could negotiate, from a position of strength, better terms and conditions with their customers and suppliers than they would have been able to as individuals. It might also suggest that the members had appreciated that a collective approach to the market would eliminate the possibility of the larger growers deliberately or inadvertently undercutting their smaller Lea Valley colleagues when agreeing selling prices for their produce, the effects of which would have inevitably created a downward spiralling of horticultural revenue across the region.

It is probable that the demands on horticulture during the war years had alerted Lea Valley growers to the possibility of future competition from abroad, particularly as improvements in technology had brought about new and faster ways of transporting, storing and handling goods. As countries around the world recovered from their darkest hour it would not be long before new growing techniques and improved transport infrastructure systems were developed, as internal economic pressures

encouraged the overseas growers to look for fresh markets and also to exploit post-war shortages. Now it was time for Lea Valley growers to consider making efficiency improvements and also to explore new ways of expanding their industry. The Council minutes of 19th February 1919 allow us an insight into members' forward thinking as a resolution from the Construction Sub Committee was submitted "That a deputation from the Lea Valley, which shall include Mr J Jody and Mr Kempston Dyson be asked to visit Holland to report on the methods of construction, heating and working of glasshouses in that country". After discussion it was agreed "...on the desirability of a deputation to Holland as soon as possible". Further discussion took place and it was proposed that each member should pay his own expenses.

Holland was one of a handful of countries that had remained neutral throughout the war and its horticultural industry had stayed largely intact maintaining good levels of food production, some of which was sold to Germany making a number of its growers rich. Naturally this had caused resentment in some quarters.

Also, at the 12th February meeting, it was proposed and agreed that the Chamber of Horticulture be informed that "in the opinion of this Association, some apprehension or restriction of imported glasshouse produce is necessary during the summer season (May to October) as, during that period, all the necessary hot-house fruits can be produced in this country, provided the necessary tariff protection and facilities for extending the industry are given". This is a clear sign that the Lea Valley Growers' Association members were beginning to flex their collective muscle and were starting to take cautious steps to protect their industry, through legislation, from cheap foreign imports and the dumping of produce. However, this would be a battle that, once commenced, would last for generations with the growers always remaining at a disadvantage as the public in general have traditionally been more interested in the lowest price rather than where the produce was grown.

Further evidence of the growers' drive towards efficiency and modernity can be gained from the Council minutes of March 1919 when it was announced that a demonstration of a Drake & Fletcher tomato-grading machine would take place at the nursery of Glasspool and Harnett. However, it was pointed out that if grading machines were to be adopted throughout the Lea Valley horticultural industry then electricity supplies would have to be connected to a number of nurseries in outlying areas. There had already been discussions with the North

Metropolitan Electric Power Supply Company about the inadequacy of electricity supplies to these remote growers, but before anything could be done to connect the nurseries an approach to Parliament would have to be made. Fortunately the subject was already before the House of Commons and the meeting requested the secretary to write to all local Members of Parliament, General Colvin, Colonel Bowles and Noel Pemberton Billing asking them to support the Bill, which if passed, would extend the present electricity network to remote areas around London. As an added precaution to make sure that the electricity company was fully aware of the locations of all the outlying nurseries the meeting agreed that the Sub Committee should have the authority to spend up to five pounds on local maps. It would appear that the initiatives taken by the growers met with success as we learn from the Council minutes of May 14th that the secretary reported "progress of the installation of electric current in the Carterhatch Road district".

In the Report of the eighth Annual General Meeting, held in October 1919, it is recorded that during the year the Lea Valley growers received two visits from outside bodies, one from a party of seventy growers from West Sussex who were guests of the Association at luncheon and another from a deputation of growers from Guernsey. These visits would suggest that the Lea Valley was now recognised as an important region of British horticulture where growers came to have mutual exchanges of information and learn new techniques. However, one cannot help wondering if there was not a slight hint of industrial espionage attached to such visits.

It was not all business and work for the Lea Valley Growers' Association as in 1919, for the first time in the post-war period, saw the return to the annual dinner, an event which had been voluntarily suspended during the wartime austerity measures. Judging by the range of fare on offer, which included dishes such as oysters, sole, chicken, veal, beef and York ham, it is fair to conclude that wartime rationing was well and truly over. Interestingly the dinner was held at the Great Eastern Hotel, Liverpool Street owned by the railway company that the Association was constantly at odds with over freight costs and late and lost deliveries. Perhaps the decision to hold the function there had something to do with the growers being able to negotiate a good price!

The Council minutes of December 1919 allow us a glimpse of how Lea Valley growers were having to wrestle with certain employment issues of the day that were particularly sensitive as some of these related to veterans of the recent war. It would appear that there had been,

as the minute quaintly put it, "a misconception" at the local Labour Exchange over the number of disabled men employed by the horticultural industry. This was thought to have been because "so few members had filled in and returned the official forms sent to them". The secretary was instructed to apply for 150 of these forms and to send them with a covering letter to all members asking that they be filled in and returned to the authorities "on the recommendation of the Council". This latter instruction would imply that members should take the matter seriously. A further instruction was given to the secretary that he should write to a Mr Hobbs (presumably an official at the local Labour Exchange) and point out "that if any disabled men who were engaged in the nursery industry before the war were in search of employment would he give us notice of same and we would do all we could to find suitable employment for these men". However, it was agreed by Council that they "could not recommend the wholesale employment of disabled men who previously belonged to some other industry or trade or no trade at all". How many of us today, when reading newspaper articles or receiving news reports on our radios and televisions, have encountered similar stories relating to the employment of disabled people? This would seem to suggest that almost one hundred years later our society has yet to solve this age-old and recurring dilemma.

For some months the minutes of the Association had recorded a number of references to Whitley Councils although there had been no real commitment from the horticultural industry to become involved with these bodies, apart from generally monitoring the situation as it developed. In 1917, during the war, John Henry Whitley had been appointed the chairman of a committee that produced a *Report on the Relations of Employers and Employees* which was designed to encourage improvements in industrial relations, a necessity for Britain in maintaining the war effort. The creation of the Whitley Councils, which are very much alive today in the public sector, allows for regular formal meetings between employers and employees to settle employment issues including the recurring question of annual pay, hours and holidays.

From the Council minutes of January 1920 we see, for the first time, the signs of unease as members try to get to grips with the realities of a Whitley Council being set up for the horticultural industry. During discussions it was proposed to "call a full Council meeting at once if in the opinion of the Labour Sub Committee the situation warranted such a course and that no overtures be made to labour representatives as yet". The ultra sensitivity of the matter can be seen when the meeting agreed to "let the question of a Whitley Council develop on its own lines in the hands of the Ministry of Labour and that no reminders be sent to the Ministry".

On 26th February a Special General Meeting of the Association was held, attended by 87 members, to discuss terms and conditions of employment for horticultural workers. It would appear that the meeting had been called to respond to an unspecified demand from the Lea Valley Council of the British Gardeners Association (BGA), later to be renamed the National Union of Horticultural Workers, a body that claimed to have "the backing of 95% of the nursery workers". After much discussion it was agreed that "ordinary nursery hands should be paid a minimum of one shilling (five pence) per hour for the legal hours of 48 in winter and 50 in summer and that overtime on weekdays should be paid for at the rate of time and a quarter and overtime on Sundays at time and a half". Over the following months a delegation of the Association met with representatives of the BGA and apart from agreeing to an improved scale of wages above that of fifty shillings per week specifically for workers who were classified as skilled, the new general terms and conditions appear to have been accepted. Before the negotiations had taken place the basic hours worked in the nurseries were 54 in the summer and 50 during the winter months.

While it may not at first appear obvious, the formulation of a standard wages structure throughout the Lea Valley horticultural industry, although slightly more costly for the employers, would bring about a greater fairness in the costs of production between the larger and smaller growers. This is an essential ingredient in keeping the local horticultural industry competitive in the face of increasingly aggressive competition from overseas growers.

It would appear that the relationship between the Association and the recently named National Union of Horticultural Workers had become quite cordial as the May 1920 Council minutes of the Association record that the secretary was instructed to write to Mr J W Craig, treasurer of the Union, to "congratulate the Horticultural Workers Union on their enterprise in starting crop growing under glass, wish them every success and state that if the Association can be of any assistance to them in any way, only too pleased to help". This entry in the minutes seems to imply that members of the Union had independently set up some form of nursery facility, perhaps with the view of growing produce that could be sold cheaply to the membership.

By October 1920, only five months after believing that things were looking up for the Lea Valley horticultural industry, the spectre of unemployment raised its head and was causing considerable concern amongst the growers. This prompted the calling a Special General Meeting of the Association on 13th October where the problem was discussed in depth. This culminated in a proposal that members be asked to send in a list of "all men discharged since 1st July". Following this a further resolution was proposed "that the Association promises to take on as many extra men as possible for winter employment in order to absorb the bona-fide nursery workers now out of work, married men and single men with dependents to be given preference to single men without dependents". Also it was agreed to contact the Union and ask them to provide a list of some 200 men thought to be out of work and it was further agreed that that an advertisement be placed in the "local newspaper and public notices be issued asking men to register themselves with the Association".

By any standard this was an impressive gesture by the Association, not just to help those nursery workers and their families who might be suffering the effects of poverty, but also as a long-sighted attempt to preserve the skills of those workers who were crucial to the survival of the Lea Valley horticultural industry before their expertise was lost forever. It is probable that the growers were aware of the fate suffered by other nearby Lea Valley industries like the Royal Small Arms Factory (RSAF) at Enfield Lock which had seen the recurring loss of skilled men, many never returning, even in better-off times, to take up their manufacturing trades again. This phenomenon always followed the inevitable decline in arms production that normally took place at the end of Britain's various conflicts.

The Council minutes of February 1921 record the setting up of a six man Sub Committee to discuss the marketing of Lea Valley produce. This initiative had probably been taken to examine ways of improving the sales revenue of the growers as later meeting minutes reveal that the nurseries were suffering increasing pressures on their markets from overseas producers. The seriousness of the situation can be gauged from the minutes of the March Council meeting when it was revealed that in the face of mounting overseas competition growers had taken around seventy-five acres of grape, growing under glass, out of production and switched their attention to other crops. There was further bad news for the Lea Valley horticultural industry when figures were released regarding the cost of growing tomatoes which had increased by approximately one hundred and ten percent since 1913, while the outlay for cucumber production had risen by more than two hundred percent during the same period. Most of these escalations had been attributed to the increased cost of labour and also the many hikes in the price of coal, an essential fuel for the glasshouse industry that was trying hard to compete with those overseas growers who had a free and plentiful supply of solar power at their disposal.

Over the next nine months the minutes of the various committees give few clues to the progress of the marketing initiatives that were under investigation to combat the effects of foreign competition. There had, however, been progress in setting up a new management and wage structure so that the administration of both the Association and the Experimental and Research Station could come under one roof. Also it can be deduced that there were continuing underlying tensions between the growers and the workforce over the thorny issues of wages and working hours. The employers seeming to take a cautious approach by not immediately responding to Union correspondence and putting off negotiations with workforce representatives for as long as possible.

We see the first signs of organised positive action against foreign competition in the minutes of a Special General Meeting held on 31 January 1922. The meeting was attended by 136 delegates from the horticultural industry and 17 attendees were from Sussex and other parts of Britain. Here several proposals were agreed, the most ambitious of them was for the Association to "invite support from all growers in the British Isles" and that a voluntary contribution of one penny per strike would be requested.

The term 'strike', although probably referring to a quantity of something, was unfamiliar to me so clarification was sought with current members of the Association. Unfortunately, the term was unfamiliar to younger members too so another avenue of enquiry was sought. Through my local contacts I was guided towards Christopher South, the great grandson of the famous Lea Valley plant pot manufacturer Samuel South (1853–1918) of Tottenham and son of Jim South, who owned Oak Nursery at Goffs Oak from 1936–1952. Christopher was a mine of information and welcomed the opportunity of recalling childhood memories of his father's nursery business. He explained that, to his knowledge, the word strike was used in the nursery industry, in the "30s, 40s, and 50s, maybe the 60s, as a volume measure used for tomatoes. It was also the name of the basket into which newly picked tomatoes were placed before being sorted, graded and packed into boxes or crates for market". Christopher further explained that "we called the basket

a strike, never a strike basket". He then went on to say "the baskets, of which every nursery had large numbers, were cylindrical, about 9 or 10 inches high and about 15 inches across, woven of fairly heavy willow with a more heavily woven lip for strength". As far as Christopher could recall, each basket held half a bushel of fruit and the word strike was only used for tomatoes.

It was also agreed that "advertising should be done this season" and consideration was to be given to a scheme for the industry to use a non-returnable tomato box. This latter suggestion would seem to be a reasonable approach towards an improved marketing plan as it is likely that a policy of non-returnable packaging would allow the British growers to compete directly with their overseas counterparts on at least one aspect of costs relating to shipping. It would be logical for overseas growers not to want to shoulder the added outlay of having their tomato packaging returned, so this particular aspect would have initially given them an advantage in the battle of competitive produce pricing. This particular aspect would seem to be one crucial, yet significant part, of determining end-product price and it is therefore surprising that there is nothing recorded in the minutes that would have given growers a breakdown of the costs or the savings that might be had so that a considered judgement could be made over the possible efficiencies and benefits with regard to the previous scheme that was currently in operation.

In March 1922 a Special General Meeting of the Association was held to formalise the setting up of a nationwide body to represent British growers. It was hoped that by coming together and having a coordinated marketing and advertising strategy the growers could begin the task of tackling foreign competition head-on. The new organisation was to go by what would no doubt today be considered an awkward-sounding name for a company involved in the business of marketing. The title was to be the British Glasshouse Produce Marketing Association Limited (BGPMA) and to this body the Lea Valley Growers' Association elected eight members to serve on the management committee. It was also agreed that the Association would donate a start-up fee of £100 to the new body, providing that this would be returned when the organisation was up and running.

The first evidence of the work of the BGPMA is recorded in the minutes of a Special General Meeting of the Association held on 28th April 1922 when it was proposed that a cucumber advertising campaign be initiated. Attending the meeting was a Mr F W Wright of the London Press Exchange who "gave an account of the advertising campaign for cucumbers". Unfortunately details of how the public might be coaxed into buying British cucumbers were not communicated through the minutes. However, the minute secretary gives us a flavour of the business through his careful choice of words. Referring to the debate which took place after Mr Wright's talk, he observed that "several members took part". And then, when recording the decision to go ahead with the advertising campaign, he wearily records "Eventually, [a very telling word for anyone who has ever attended a business meeting] on the motion of Mr H B Randall seconded by Mr J Harnett, it was agreed with one dissentient that this meeting endorsed the action of the Committee of Management of the BGPMAL in inaugurating a Cucumber Advertising and Publicity Campaign. This concluded the business". Considering the pressures on the growers from overseas competition there does appear to be a certain lack of dynamism and urgency about the fight-back by the British horticultural industry.

When viewing, from a distance, the decision-making process of many organisations, including central and local government, particularly when urgent remedial action is required, (the Lea Valley Growers' Association being no exception), the democratic process can often appear laboured and cumbersome as committees take time in deliberating what actions might or should be taken that could eventually bring about a satisfactory outcome. To an outsider the situation can often be likened to a case of someone haemorrhaging to death and a committee being set up to debate, and then vote, on a motion as to whether a tourniquet or a bandage should be applied as the most effective form of treatment.

The first inkling of an advertising campaign occurs when at a Special General Meeting was held on the afternoon of Thursday 22nd June at St Mary's Hall, Cheshunt. The meeting seems to have been called for the sole purpose of showing members an advertising film with the rather risqué title of *The Love Apple*. The term "Love Apple" refers to the humble tomato, which some had once thought to be an aphrodisiac, but I am sure such racy thoughts were not behind the title for the film! No further details were recorded about the advertising campaign and there was only a request from members to see the film again. In the days before television the general public would have watched the film at the cinema which, at the time, was a popular place of entertainment.

The next occasion when the advertising campaign is mentioned is in the minutes of the Special General Meeting of January 1923; when the secretary was asked "to give an account of the advertising campaign conducted during 1922". Frustratingly all we are able learn is that the secretary reported, "several questions were asked and answered by members of the Committee of Management of the BGPMAL"; no details of how the campaign was to be structured or the target audience the campaign was to be aimed at were forthcoming. However, we learn that the chairman called on members to "enrol" for the 1923 campaign at £20 per acre or six shillings and eight pence per 100 "strikes" (see explanation above for this term) in the case of tomatoes and one penny per "flat" in the case of cucumbers. It would seem that many of the members present must have thought that the 1922 campaign was worthwhile and successful as after the chairman's call for members to enrol for the 1923 campaign it is recorded that "a large number of forms were signed".

Throughout the year there are various references in the minutes to workmen's wages, holiday pay and weekly hours and the impression gained is that no one really wanted to deal with the matter particularly urgently. Even after a special meeting in March when the growers discussed the matter the decision taken was to leave things as they were for the time being. However, agreement was finally reached to review the situation on a six-monthly basis and at the 1923 September General Meeting of Trade Members a full schedule of terms and conditions was published as follows:

1. Minimum Hourly Rate of Pay for capable and experienced Male Nursery Workers over 21 years of age, 10d. per hour.

2. Minimum Weekly Rate of 48 hours at 10d. per hour. i.e. 40s. to be guaranteed.

3. Saturday Afternoon and Sunday Work.
   After 1 p.m. on Saturdays and all Sunday time at one and a quarter times the ordinary hourly rate.

4. Bank Holidays.

(a) Employees working till 1 p.m. on Bank Holidays to receive a full ordinary day's pay.

(b) All time worked after 1 p.m. on Bank Holidays to be paid for at one and a quarter times the ordinary hourly rate of pay in addition to the ordinary pay mentioned in (a).

The schedule was to be circulated by the secretary to all members and it was recommended that it should take effect from 6th October that year. There does not appear to have been any consultation with the workforce representatives regarding the agreement of the schedule, something that is normally taken for granted in all well-run twenty-first-century industries. During the year the workers' trade union representative had written to the Association requesting the reinstatement of the Conciliation Committee but the request was turned down. In February 1924 the Association received another letter from the workers' trade union asking once more for the Conciliation Committee to be re-established and this time the secretary was instructed to reply with the following answer which is extremely firm and direct: "The Council of the Association has carefully considered your letter of February 28th and is unable to recommend the members of the Association to make any variation in the present conditions of employment in the industry. Further correspondence on the subject would be useless".

One might question if this was a sensible approach as it would have been logical for all personnel within the horticultural industry to remain strong and united in the face of growing foreign competition. Industrial harmony would seem to be a desirable goal with a good day-to-day working relationship between growers and workforce and having a committee where concerns of both employer and employee could be aired and shared would have gone some way to achieving that and would have been a reasonable way of heading off potential future problems.

Wages were not the only costs concerning the Association. During this period the various minutes record battles with the Great Eastern Railway over freight charges and also late deliveries and there are disputes with the Covent Garden Market authorities over being charged one half penny per quarter bushel for market toll with respect of tomatoes when it is alleged that "according to the Charter of the Market they are only entitled to charge one half penny per bushel and so on in proportion of larger and smaller quantities". Things had obviously come to a head as the secretary was instructed to write to the Ministry of Agriculture and the Controller of Horticulture to bring the matter to their attention.

The secretary was also instructed to write to these two bodies "to draw their attention to the fact that the Market Authorities had threatened, unofficially, to take drastic action against any salesman or grower who attempted to remedy this gross injustice and further to ask the Ministry of Agriculture and the Controller of Horticulture to take the matter in hand on behalf of the whole industry".

It will be recalled that at the general meeting in January 1922, in an effort to compete more aggressively with foreign growers, it was agreed that non-returnable packaging for tomatoes should be introduced. Therefore, it is somewhat surprising to discover a reference in the minutes of a special meeting, held at Cheshunt on 10th October 1923 of the Covent Garden Conference Delegates, that a Mr Munro should be approached to speak about "In what way can we improve the marketing of Tomatoes for the future with special reference to the use of Non-returnable Boxes?" Interestingly Mr Munro was to be asked to give his talk immediately after the Annual General Meeting of the Association on 31st October. This is almost two years after the non-returnable tomato box had been agreed as part of a marketing campaign to fight foreign competition.

As an outsider looking back at the progress of Lea Valley growers from almost one hundred years into the future one cannot help but conclude that the demise of the horticultural industry did not occur after the Second World War. By a cursory examination of the growers' collective businesses the tell-tale signs, that would eventually lead to shrinkage of the Lea Valley horticultural industry, were appearing much earlier in the century and were there for all to see.

While the Association had been set up as a democratic model and in the early years had gone about its tasks with speed and efficiency, as it grew, a plethora of sub-committees had emerged that covered anything from lectures and social events to transport and finance and from the investigation of manures to the manufacture of chutney. These sub-committees would be passed various projects to investigate by the main meetings of the Association and it was quite usual to see many months elapse before a recommendation was passed back to the original issuing body for further consideration. The whole process was time consuming and cumbersome and tied the Association's hands with regard to responding quickly on issues such as foreign competition that needed constant and immediate attention. One can only wonder how many other British industries operated in a similar way and whether this was one of the reasons why we, as a country, have failed to capitalise on the technological progress made after the start of the industrial revolution. There are other observations made when reading the various meeting minutes that have concerned the author.

The same names keep cropping up in the framing and proposing of resolutions and it is these same names, probably those of the larger growers who may have had more time, that are the ones whom the meetings regularly put forward to represent the Association on external bodies and also with regard to negotiations with government departments and other organisations. While it may not be an intentional or conscious wish on behalf of those who serve in these areas, it does however place considerable power, by way of knowledge and external contact, in the hands of the few. This makes these representatives the Association's experts in the eyes of the members and guarantees them more external nominations.

Perhaps a better way of organising the Lea Valley Growers' Association would have been to have appointed a small dedicated team of professionals, paid for out of a general levy. For the scheme to work, the team would have needed to be given a certain amount of autonomy, allowing them the ability to move quickly to make important decisions on behalf of the Association. It would be the task of the Association to direct the team allowing them to focus on specific business targets and other important issues, while allowing the growers to do what they did best, cultivate produce.

Towards the end of 1923 and the beginning of 1924 the minutes of the General Meeting of the Association record, for the first time, employees from the Lea Valley nurseries being invited to attend a meeting with the growers. However, these meetings were not intended to discuss the general business of the Association, they were for the purpose of receiving lectures concerning subjects of general interest to the nursery industry such as the growing and propagation of crops, the boring of wells and the heating of glasshouses. The turnout at one of these early meetings was some fifty growers and between ninety and one hundred employees.

Also at about this time another new initiative was introduced which was specifically designed to encourage employers and employees to come up with new ideas that would be beneficial to the horticultural industry. The reader will not be surprised to learn that a special Prizes Sub-Committee was appointed to work out the details that would satisfy the aims of the initiative. This culminated in a recommendation to the December 1923 Council Meeting of the Association to hold a competition, the working of which is set out as follows:

"Class. (I) For some meritorious mechanical contribution towards the advancement of the industry.

Class. (II) For the best essay on Glasshouse Culture, Construction or any other subject appertaining to the Glasshouse Industry.

The competitions to be open to both employers and employees. The award to be a certificate of merit and a cheque for £5. 5. 0 or in the opinion of the winner a cup or medal in each case. All entries to be sent to the secretary by September 29th 1924".

Remembering the total resistance of the growers to forming a Conciliation Committee that could have created a platform for employer and employee to discuss common issues; was the proposal for an annual competition, that invited both sides to come up with new and imaginative ideas to materially improve the horticultural industry, an informal attempt by the Association to unblock what had become an industry stalemate, or was it a veiled admission of strained industrial relations?

An Emergency General Meeting of the Association was called on 22nd August 1924 to discuss a strike of the workmen at Covent Garden Market which was causing the Lea Valley Growers considerable problems with the distribution of their produce. The upshot was that a resolution was proposed which, in no uncertain terms, reflected the mood of the meeting as follows, "That this meeting of the Lea Valley Growers gives its unanimous support to the employers in Covent Garden Market in opposing all attempts to increase the costs of marketing

Covent Garden Market at the beginning of the 20th century. Some of the carts are loaded with tomato baskets (strikes).

which they consider are already excessive. Should these expenses be increased, the Growers will be compelled to use Covent Garden as little as possible and continue distributing their produce direct to the provinces as they have been doing during the past week".

Unfortunately we learn absolutely nothing with regard to the nature of the response to the Association's letter. The Council minutes of the Association for the 10th September only record a fleeting reference that, "Mr John Poupart gave a brief account of the present position in Covent Garden Market". Sadly this is a fairly typical example of the problems that I have regularly encountered throughout the writing of this book. Of course if one had unlimited time and money it might be possible for a researcher to access the archives of Covent Garden Market to see if any relevant material still exists but it is doubtful. Should anything eventually be discovered it would probably not add much to the story.

The members' and workers' enthusiasm for entering the essay and mechanical devices competition had clearly been disappointing as we learn from the October Council Meeting that only a few essays had been received and just one letter relating to a mechanical device. However, three judges were appointed and agreed to announce their decisions at the Annual General Meeting on 28th October. Unfortunately their decision had to be deferred to a later date as the lone competitor had not given sufficient information about his mechanical device. At a meeting on 16th December a Mr Frank Russell read his essay on "Some Points in Connection with Tomato Growing" which had been judged as worth the five guinea first prize and a Mr H W Hollis, of the Institute, Turnford, received the runner up prize of two guineas for his essay entitled "Tomato Culture". There was no mention of what happened to the prize for the mechanical device although the members agreed that the competition for both categories of prize should continue for another year.

On a number of occasions throughout 1924 the growers had raised their concerns over the price and delivery of coal and also the facilities being offered at the local railway stations regarding the storage and transfer of this extremely essential commodity. In an effort to resolve the matter a joint conference was called for 27th November 1924 between representatives of the Association and representatives of the coal industry. The fact that the meeting was held at Elm Arches, Turners Hill, Cheshunt, gives an indication of how powerful and influential the Lea Valley Growers' Association had

become, particularly as representatives of some of the coal merchants had travelled from as far afield as Birmingham and Swansea.

During the conference a "long and friendly discussion took place" between members of the Association and representatives of the coal industry and it was apparent that both sides had agreed that the railway company was to blame for the continuing frustrations of the growers. The item of major debate concerned problems with the siding accommodation and the unloading of wagons at Cheshunt, Theobalds Grove, Broxbourne, and Rye House railway stations. The coal industry representatives and the growers had a mutual interest in resolving this matter and it is clear that the timing of the conference was quite deliberate and had been called to gather information which would be used to confront managers of the London & North Eastern Railway Company (formerly the Great Eastern Railway Company) ahead of their meeting with the growers at the Association's Council Meeting at Cheshunt on 10th December. The minutes of the 10th December Council Meeting record little information about the discussion that took place only saying that the representatives of the railway company, Mr P Syden and Mr E J Burrows, "should get additional information showing the clearances by individual members of our Association at these local stations and attend a further meeting of the Council on January 14th 1925". In fact this meeting was a bit of a disappointment as it was reported that Mr Syden could not attend "as he had not yet collected all the information which would be necessary before a consultation with the Council would result in useful action". This probably meant that his colleagues at the London & North Eastern Railway Company had not been forthcoming with information or perhaps Mr Syden was playing for time.

While the Association was awaiting information from the railway company the issue of reinstating the Conciliation Committee raised its head once again. This time it was not the glasshouse workers' representative that was calling the shots, but was the Hertfordshire Wages Committee who had issued an ultimatum under the Agricultural Wages (Regulation) Act, 1924. The Council Meeting of 29th January 1925 "discussed the matter from every point of view" and then resolved to recommend to the General Meeting which followed "that the suggested reformation of a Conciliation Committee be disapproved".

After receiving the recommendations of the Council the General Meeting unanimously agreed a resolution "that this Meeting of the Lea Valley Growers is of opinion that the reconstitution of a Conciliation Committee would not be in the best interests of the employers and employees of the glasshouse industry". It was also unanimously agreed that the Association's solicitor be asked to arrange representation for the growers at the Hertfordshire Wages Committee on 7th February. While the minutes never disclose why the Lea Valley Growers were vehemently opposed to the establishment of a Conciliation Committee it would seem pretty obvious that they were against the concept of a standardised minimum wage for the horticultural industry, particularly if it was being imposed by an external body. Individual growers preferred the flexibility of setting the hourly rates of pay for their employees individually. Mr J P Rochford, a leading light in the opposition to the Conciliation Committee, was unanimously co-opted as a member of the Council "in order to deal with problems arising out of the Agricultural Wages Act 1924, as a delegate of the Association in that matter". It would now appear that the Association had drawn battle lines and was preparing for a fight.

At the Council Meeting of 11th February the secretary reported that he had received two letters from the Association's solicitor. Although we have no idea of their content it would be reasonable to assume that the solicitor had made the suggestion that a special Conference should be convened to allow the glasshouse industry to discuss the various issues regarding the Hertfordshire Wages Committee. The Council Meeting went along with the Conference idea and recommended that representatives from the National Farmers Union headquarters, the Hertfordshire Branch of the Farmers Union, the Middlesex Branch of the Farmers Union, the Chamber of Horticulture, the Federation of British Horticultural Trades Association, the British Florists' Federation, the Home Counties Growers' Association, the east Sussex Growers' Association and the North West Kent Growers' Association, should be invited to discuss their concerns regarding the recent ultimatum of the Hertfordshire Wages Committee. It was further suggested that each of these bodies should be invited to send one or two representatives.

Interestingly there is more than a touch of irony in the wording of the Council Meeting minute when the secretary details the members' reasons for inviting so many different organisations to the proposed Conference. The reasons given is, "in order that the issues involved might be thoroughly discussed by a representative body comprising all sections of the nursery, market garden, glasshouse and agricultural industries together with such other growers as the secretary might consider desirable

for the purpose of obtaining a thoroughly representative opinion". To have "a thoroughly representative opinion", would surely have required at least one representative from the workman's trade union?

In the meantime Mr Syden of the railway company had again attended the Council Meeting to discuss the proposed increase in siding accommodation at Cheshunt Station "giving certain facts and figures which had been supplied to him by the railway servants in regard to the number of trucks placed at Cheshunt Station for clearance on certain days and the number of trucks cleared on the same days". The figures did not impress the members and Mr Syden was told, probably in no uncertain terms, that they "did not bear any direct relation to the facts in their own particular cases". One cannot help but feel sorry for this poor man, who has been placed in the impossible position of go-between and all he could do was promise to look into the figures once more and report back to the Association.

The next chapter in the Conciliation Committee debate was at a meeting at the National Farmers Union (NFU), Bedford Square, London Headquarters on 20th February 1925, attended by members of the Association's Council. After considerable debate, the President of the National Farmers Union, Mr Rowland Robbins expressed the view that he regarded the Association's idea to call a Conference of the different agricultural and horticultural bodies "with apprehension". Robbins had shrewdly recognised something that the Lea Valley Growers' Association had completely overlooked in their quest to isolate the trade union representative of the workers and he was able to convince the meeting that a Conference representing the many horticultural and agricultural organisations nationally was a bad idea.

The Association members grasped the logic of the argument presented and "unanimously agreed that owing to the fact that the Hertfordshire Wages Committee were not really concerned with fixing a rate for "commercial horticulture" generally but more particularly were concerned with fixing a special rate for "glasshouse workers" in the South East corner of Hertfordshire, that a special memorandum on the subject of the "glasshouse workers" be submitted to the Hertfordshire Wages Committee at their next meeting on March 21st". Now determined to get things right the Council members of the Association agreed to reconvene a special meeting at the Headquarters of the NFU on 6th March to ensure that the memorandum was correctly drafted. At this meeting Mr Robbins argued that the Association should "try to re-establish the Conciliation Committee while they had the opportunity". While his suggestion was accepted "nem con" and would now go before an Emergency General Meeting of the Association on 11th March, some Council members were still uncomfortable with the idea as two had left the meeting before the vote could be taken and two others abstained. When the resolution "that the Association does now agree to the suggestion of the Chairman of the Hertfordshire Wages Committee to re-form a Conciliation Committee subject to the proviso that the six workers' representatives are bona fide' glasshouse employees engaged in the Lea Valley" was put to the Association's members at the Emergency Meeting it was carried by thirty-one votes to seven with eleven abstentions. Six Council members were appointed to serve on the Conciliation Committee. However, when reading the minutes, one cannot help but feel that there was still not a great deal of enthusiasm for the idea.

At the Council Meeting on 8th April 1925, after the report of the Conciliation Committee representatives was discussed, it was unanimously agreed to recommend the adoption of a "slightly modified" wages and hourly schedule of work as follows. For "capable and experienced male nursery workers" over twenty one years of age, the minimum hourly rate would be 10d (4.16 pence in today' money) and the normal working week would consist of fifty-four hours. A minimum weekly rate of forty-eight hours at 10d per hour would be guaranteed. Overtime at one and a quarter times the ordinary hourly rate would be paid for work in excess of fifty-four hours worked previous to 1pm on Saturdays and the same rate to be paid after 1pm on Saturdays and also for all Sunday time. Employees working on public holidays up to 1pm (this changed to 12 noon one month later) to receive an ordinary day's pay and time worked after 1pm to be paid at one and a quarter times hourly rate.

After the meeting had accepted the new scale of employees' terms and conditions another motion was unanimously agreed "that no graduated scale for those below twenty-one years of age should be recognised". Just when it was looking as though progress was being made on the industrial relations front the Council members had put this harsh condition on the new scales that had been jointly agreed by the Conciliation Committee. While it is possible that the Committee had failed to consider this potential loop-hole in the schedule, the Council members, by wishing to impose such a condition would seem not to be acting in the spirit of the recommendation. The members also unanimously agreed to leave the question of annual holidays to the discretion of individual growers.

Throughout the rest of 1925 and also during 1926 there are motions, letters and also involvement of the Association's solicitors with regard to disputes with the Hertfordshire Wages Committee. Although the information recorded in the Association's minutes is often scant and cryptic, making the nature of the issues unclear, it can usually be gleaned that the central bone of contention is employee wage rates. At the Council Meeting of 8th December 1926 the President, Vice President and Chairman are asked to draft a letter to the Hertfordshire Wages Committee "emphasising the fact that the Lea Valley Growers are still dissatisfied with the working of the Agricultural Wages Order". Given this continuing long-term sniping by the Association it would seem that despite the re-instatement of the Conciliation Committee the differences between the employers and the employees would not be resolved easily and the issues were set to run and run.

Also throughout the 1925/1926 period there is continuing correspondence, meetings and visits between the Association and representatives of the London & North Eastern Railway Company over ongoing unresolved complaints of late produce deliveries to the markets around Britain. Also, there were accommodation and storage issues at local Lea Valley railway stations which had yet to be resolved. Ironically, even after all the contact and communication from the Association, the growers learned, through press reports (June 1926), that the railway company planned to update the facilities at Cheshunt, Broxbourne and Rye House Stations. As might be imagined the news did not go down well with the growers and the secretary was yet again instructed to write to the railway company. This he did by alluding to the press report and making the point that "we trust this would include all stations in the Lea Valley district".

The seemingly dilatory response by the railway company to the growers requests for improved local facilities so that produce could be handled more efficiently is difficult to understand. For as early as 1879, the Great Eastern Railway Company had opened its own fruit and vegetable market at Burford Road, on the south side of Stratford High Street, East London, which at the time was a state-of-the-art complex. The facilities consisted of two lines of warehouses two hundred and twenty yards long that were separated by a forty-foot roadway, with railway lines running along the back of each row of buildings so that produce could be loaded directly into storage. Capacity was such that the designers claimed that two hundred trucks could be unloaded simultaneously. The long warehouses were divided into separate units and the railway company leased these out

The former Stratford Vegetable Market, Burford Road.

Food lorry being escorted by armoured car during the General Strike of 1926.

to various businesses connected with the wholesale and retail fruit and vegetable trade.

It is known that the Lea Valley Growers had dealings with the Stratford Market as the Council Minutes of 10th June, 1925 allude to, "provision of truck and warehouse accommodation for a certain salesman at Stratford". One would have thought that because the railway company had direct experience of handling perishable products in their own right, they would have responded more speedily to the growers' requests. Perhaps there could be an explanation as it is known that the railway company was dealing with businesses in Hamburg and Holland and in later years an express train would arrive at Stratford in the early hours of the morning bringing produce from the Continent via the Harwich-Zeebrugge ferry. Because the Continental growers were in competition with their Lea Valley counterparts, and would have been important railway customers, could it be that an 'understanding' had been arranged with the railway management?

Looking at the whole railway episode and the continuing niggling wages disputes of the growers, from the position of the twenty-first century, it is hard to believe that Britain had, compared with today, a relatively strong industrial economy. Therefore, the question has to be asked, were these particular issues a microcosm of a greater set of underlying problems which would lead to our eventual economic difficulties?

The year 1926 was a memorable one not only for the Lea Valley Growers who agreed, at their October Annual General Meeting to become a Branch of the National Farmers' Union, but also for all of Britain, whose transport system was plunged into chaos when the General Strike began on 4th May. The reasons for the dispute are complex and have their roots in 1924 when the coal

owners agreed to increase the wages of the coal miners. In 1925 the government of the day re-adopted the gold standard and set the exchange rate for the pound sterling against the American dollar at the higher pre-war rate, rather than the lower level that it had reached. This resulted in making exports uncompetitive, causing a fall in industrial output. The knock-on effect for employers was to see their profit margins reduced and they therefore demanded a return to lower wages. The Miners Federation refused to accept such terms and the stage was set for the dispute to escalate. However, the miners were at a distinct disadvantage in any future negotiation as there were relatively large stocks of coal available. The miners' leaders appealed to the General Council of the Trade Union Congress and in July 1925 the Railwaymen and the Transport Workers placed an embargo upon the movement of coal.

The General Strike ended in confusion only nine days after it had begun. In his analysis of the dispute, labour historian Henry Pelling blames certain trade union leaders for its collapse as they had failed, in their negotiations, to wring any concessions out of government. Sadly the effects of the strike are still felt to this day, as resentment remains between small groups of families living within mining villages. Also it has left lingering divisions across the mining community. The reasons for these lasting emotions emanates from stories of those mining ancestors who crossed picket lines, the absolute transgression for any trade unionist, being passed down the generations. These feelings were reinforced in recent years by the miners' strike of 1984–1985.

Of course the General Strike had caused serious problems for Lea Valley growers. The country still had to be fed and the lack of public transport meant that produce could not be moved to the markets around Britain via the railway network. Fortunately, for the growers, the General Council of the Trades Union Congress had not called out the agricultural or horticultural workers, so produce could still be processed. This meant that private transport could be arranged to get the output of the nurseries to market.

As the transport difficulties caused by the General Strike were fading from the growers' memories, the minutes of the November, 1926 Council Meeting revealed a more serious problem for the Lea Valley horticultural industry to deal with. A grant of £200 for the year 1926/1927 was allocated, with little hesitation, to the Turners Hill Experimental and Research Station to find ways of combating an infestation of the red spider mite. The pest was known to be particularly virulent amongst plants grown under glass, extracting the contents of leaf cells which produced a mottling effect on the upper leaf surfaces. If not treated swiftly, the leaf can wither and drop off with the possibility of the plant eventually dying. Future Association minutes show that the growers were continually allotting substantial sums of money to the Turners Hill Experimental and Research Station to find a solution to the red spider mite infestations that seemed to occur regularly.

The year 1927 began with members of the Association being appointed to serve on three prominent bodies, the National Council of Agriculture, the National Farmers' Union Headquarters' Fruit and Vegetable Committee and the Glasshouse Growers sub-committee of the Fruit and Vegetable Sub-Committee. Being invited to serve on national bodies would suggest that the Lea Valley Growers were recognised by their peers as important players within the horticultural industry.

The possibility of establishing a canning factory in the Lea Valley was raised at the Council Meeting of 12th January by the Association's secretary who reminded the members that help for such an enterprise could be given by the Ministry of Agriculture. In fact the canning factory idea had been raised some years before as it was thought that the establishment of such a plant would have been a successful way of dealing with tomato surpluses, but this early initiative seems to have been shelved. On this later introduction of the scheme, it was proposed by Mr C H Shoults, one of the prominent Council members, and unanimously agreed by the meeting, that "under the present conditions the proposition was impracticable". The statement probably gives us an insight into the tight economic conditions that many businesses across Britain were experiencing at the time. This view is reinforced later in the year when the thirteenth annual dinner,

which was to be held in November and attended by the Minister of Agriculture, was cancelled, "owing to the very depressed condition of the industry".

It has been estimated that paying for the First World War had cost Britain twenty-five percent of her national wealth. On the horizon, less than two years away, the western industrial world was about to feel the severe economic effects of America's "Wall Street Crash", with the collapse of hundreds of banks and the wiping out of stock market shares prices. This economic meltdown would lead to a period of severe austerity named the "Great Depression" that would remain throughout the 1930s.

The next event of the growers' January calendar was a special Extraordinary General Meeting on 27th when it was unanimously agreed that the rather cumbersome title the, Lea Valley and District Nurserymen's and Growers' Association Limited, which had remained attached to the organisation since the inaugural meeting in 1911, should be changed to the more user-friendly Lea Valley Growers' Association Limited. Also, at about this time, the growers had received information that plans were afoot to move Covent Garden Market to Bloomsbury. For reasons which are not clear, the Lea Valley Growers took great exception to the proposition and then did what they usually did in such circumstances; moved a resolution. The proposer was once again Mr C H Shoults, who suggested that the following resolution should be sent to the National Farmers' Union, "That this meeting of the Lea Valley Growers considers the proposed removal of Covent Garden Market against the interests of growers and urges the National Farmers' Union to oppose the Bill".

It is impossible to learn, from the minutes, the reasons why the Association were so against the Market being relocated and it would be difficult to imagine that the growers had any thoughts of wanting to preserve Covent Garden's rich historical heritage; they probably knew very little about it. Interestingly, the area acquired its name around the thirteenth century when it was once part of arable land and orchards belonging to Westminster Abbey and referred to at the time as "the garden of the Abbey and Convent". At the dissolution of the monasteries, under King Henry VIII in 1540, the grounds were acquired by the Earls of Bedford and it was the fourth Earl who commissioned Inigo Jones to build a number of stately houses on the land. By the mid 1600s a small open air market set up in the area but it was not until the 1830s that the first neo-classical building was erected to cover the market which, by accounts, had become a disorganised sprawl. Over the years Covent Garden became Britain's largest and best known fruit and vegetable market. We now know that the proposal to move Covent Garden Market to Bloomsbury did not take place and that the suggestion was either a rumour or perhaps the Association's resolution was successful after all. As post-war congestion grew in the area of central London the authorities quickly realised that the Market's future was limited. Land was acquired at Nine Elms, Vauxhall in the early 1970s and the New Covent Garden Market was built. In 1974 the old Covent Garden Market relocated to the new address.

The Earls of Bedford acquired the grounds of Covent Garden. It was the fourth Earl who commissioned Inigo Jones to build stately homes in the area.

Over the years the Lea Valley Growers had regularly complained about the imports of cheap fruit and vegetables, particularly tomatoes, from countries such as Belgium, Holland and Spain and had tried, unsuccessfully, to get successive governments to impose an import produce tax from these countries. Had such an

New Covent Garden Market, Nine Elms, Battersea.

arrangement been implemented, it would have reduced the imports of foreign produce, allowing Lea Valley growers to sell more of their crops to the markets of Britain. Of course, the government would have been well aware of the risks of introducing such a levy on imported fruit and vegetables as the countries concerned could easily impose punitive taxes on British goods entering their respective markets.

At a Council Meeting on 14th September 1927 the matter of foreign fruit and vegetable imports was raised yet again by a Mr Carabis of Pick Hill, Waltham Abbey, and after much discussion it was pointed out to Mr Carabis that there were, "difficulties in the adoption of such a procedure as wished by him". Nevertheless, the secretary was asked to write to the three local Members of Parliament, Admiral Sir Murray Sueter, Lieutenant Colonel Reginald Aplin and the Chancellor of the Exchequer, Winston Churchill, "to ascertain their views on the matter".

A letter from Lieutenant Colonel Aplin was received in time for the October Council Meeting and although we do not know the content, the secretary was requested to write to Mr Carabis and suggest that he should introduce his import levy proposal at the November Annual General Meeting (AGM). Unfortunately Mr Carabis did not turn up at the AGM and no apology from him is recorded in the minutes of the meeting, nor did members discuss the matter in his absence. It is probably fair to speculate that, even if the growers had lobbied their Members of Parliament on the issue of import levies it would have been unlikely that the government would have wanted to risk the implementation of such a scheme, as legislation of this nature had the potential to create a tit for tat reciprocal policy by foreign governments and, as a result, British exports would have suffered.

Possessing some knowledge of the Lea Valley industries can, on occasions, be helpful when trying to make sense of the limited information contained within the early minute books of the Lea Valley Growers' Association. The task frequently proves challenging, particularly when striving to create a narrative to hold the readers interest. So when I read that complaints had been received at the February 1929 Council Meeting of "smoke nuisance at Brimsdown" from members of the Association, who presumably had nurseries in the area, I had a fair idea of what might have been going on. The minute also noted a letter had been received from the North Metropolitan Electric Power Supply Company (Northmet), the content of which we are unable to ascertain, but in referring to the letter the secretary recorded, "in view

Brimsdown B Power Station
that became the source of smoke
complaints from nurseries in 1928

of the contents of the letter it was resolved unanimously that members be asked to note any improvement or otherwise in the matter and report the result in two or three weeks time".

In 1903 the Metropolitan Electric Tramways Company placed a contract to build a power station on twelve acres of land adjacent to the Lee navigation at Brimsdown to produce power for their tram network. The following year the contract was taken over by Northmet who began a programme to expand electricity generation on the site to satisfy the requirements of the local power-hungry industries that were growing and also for new ones setting up in the region. By 1925 with the domestic market for electricity now increasing as well for industry, not to mention the Lea Valley nurseries too, the decision was taken to build a further power station, to be known as Brimsdown 'B' in support the original Brimsdown 'A'.

Building work on the station was held up for two reasons, one, due to difficulties in reaching agreement with the Metropolitan Water Board over securing water supplies for cooling purposes and, two, the circumstances surrounding the 1926 General Strike and the restricted movement of coal (see above) would have severely limited the station's output. This meant that the first section of Brimsdown 'B' was not operational until August 1928 and it was a little after the station was commissioned that complaints of "smoke nuisance" were raised by some of the growers. Therefore, it would seem fair to conclude that the increase in smoke problems had been exacerbated by the second coal-burning power station, Brimsdown 'B', coming on line.

The subject of smoke nuisance was again raised at the Growers' May Council Meeting and members reported that correspondence on the subject had appeared in *The Times* concerning the problem. Members affected were advised to keep records of the occurrences and to complain periodically to the power supply company. Members were also requested to "notify the secretary from time to time". The secretary reported that he had received information that "another body with statutory powers had taken action in relation to smoke nuisance and it was anticipated that an improvement would take place sooner or later". What is remarkable about the "smoke nuisance" story is the speed in which the matter was reported and the swiftness of the various actions. From the commissioning of Brimsdown 'B' Power Station to an entry in the Council Minutes was a period of around six months. Remembering the rather long-winded approach that the Lea Valley Growers' Association had taken towards developing a scheme to collectively market their produce (see above) it could be thought that at last the streamlining of urgent business matters were beginning to take place. However, I shall reserve my judgement until I delve further into the later sets of minutes!

The 1930s was an unsettling time not just in Britain, where the economic effects of the Great Depression were still being strongly felt, but also across the countries of Europe. The appointment of Adolf Hitler as German

Chancellor in January 1933 would soon see him ignoring the terms and conditions of the Treaty of Versailles with the implementation of a programme to rearm his country. This deliberate mark of defiance by the German Chancellor was about to threaten world stability, the effects of which would be felt across Britain as, amongst other things, she would have to reorganise her food supplies not just to feed the civilian population but also her armed forces. It was against this backdrop that the Lea Valley Growers had to operate and surprisingly the minutes of the Association give little information away with regard to the impending crisis that was soon to engulf the world in the most serious conflict ever witnessed in history. Given the momentous series of events that were about to unfold I wondered if it would be possible to place a more rounded interpretation on the Association's minutes as, although they were giving little away, they were now being written in the light of an extremely fast-moving situation?

Surprisingly, the minutes up until the mid 1930s convey nothing of the seriousness of the developing international situation and the growers seem to be more energised about arranging their forthcoming annual dinners than that of the fast-moving national and international events. The main issue concerning the growers was still the large quantities of cheap produce arriving from abroad and the wish of the Association to see a range of tariffs applied to foreign imports. Interestingly, it was the question of tariffs that had caused splits in both the Conservative and Liberal Parties at the time of the 1931 general election. Under the leadership of Stanley Baldwin the Conservatives had wanted to

David Lloyd George – a supporter of free trade.

establish a protectionist trade policy and this idea was supported by the break-away Liberal Nationals under Sir John Simon. The old Liberal Party, led by Lloyd George and Sir Herbert Samuel, campaigned in support of free trade. The 1931 and 1935 governments were both coalition and were therefore all-party, remaining this way with no more general elections until after the Second World War.

Knowing a little of the political events of the 1930s has allowed us another opportunity to make a reasonable assumption regarding the 14th October 1931 minutes of the Association when the secretary reported that "he had been asked by Mr Winston Churchill, the prospective Member of Parliament for Epping, to furnish certain figures in connection with the glasshouse industry".

Stanley Baldwin who was in favour of tariffs on imported goods.

Winston Churchill, who was Chancellor of the Exchequer when Britain returned to the gold standard.

In the sentence that followed we get one of those frustrating statements, "The secretary read to the committee the notes he had supplied to Mr Churchill which were approved". Luckily the next piece of recorded information allows us to see the wider connection when the chairman stated, "that in the event of the National Government being elected it would be desirable to present a case for a tariff on tomatoes". The meeting then unanimously agreed to refer the matter to the Executive Committee to prepare a case.

Winston Churchill had lost his seat in the 1929 general election when Stanley Baldwin's Conservative Government failed to hold their majority, resulting in a hung parliament. Their demise had mainly been caused by their poor handling of the economy and, in particular, over returning Britain to the gold standard in 1924. The depression that followed, later exacerbated by the American stock market crash in October 1929 (Wall Street crash), caused great hardship as unemployment rose as industry shed labour. The tying of the pound sterling to the pre-war gold standard had made British goods and services uncompetitive on the international market. Much of the blame for this, which was acknowledged in later life, was directed at Churchill during his period as Chancellor of the Exchequer (1924–1929), nevertheless he was returned as Member of Parliament for the Epping Constituency on 27th October 1931.

When Churchill had asked the Lea Valley Growers to, "furnish certain figures in connection with the glasshouse industry" he was clearly looking to secure their votes as he had been out of parliament for the past two years. On Churchill's return to the Commons it is probable that his strong and sometimes controversial views had negated his chances of being offered a cabinet post in Ramsay MacDonald's National Government. However, he was no doubt seen by the Lea Valley Growers as a man who could champion their cause.

From entries in the Lea Valley Growers Council minutes for November and December 1931 we see that there was considerable activity regarding the question of tariffs. A letter from a Mr E Matthews of Ponders End asked the

Crowds form outside the American Union Bank during the Great Depression of 1929.

Association if they would press for a tariff on grapes as "the grape grower was in very serious need of such protection". While the meeting agreed that this section of the horticultural industry required attention they nevertheless came to the conclusion that "it was felt desirable that the committee should concentrate on the tomato question". It would appear that growers felt the imposition of a protectionist tariff on foreign produce was the one single factor that could assist their industry, particularly at a time when the global economy was passing through a state of melt-down. The seriousness in which they took this matter can be gauged when Mr H O Larsen, President of the Association, introduced to the Council the subject of the proposed tariff on imported tomatoes and "drew attention to the charts which were displayed around the committee room". After considerable discussion it was unanimously agreed that the tariff should be set by weight and a letter of explanation, accompanied by the charts, should be sent to the National Farmers' Union, "subject to slight alteration as may be necessary" and copies of the letter should also be sent to "other Glasshouse Associations".

The minutes of the December Council meeting confirm that tariffs had been agreed with other Glasshouse Associations and although there had been correspondence over the inclusion of peaches it was decided that this product "would probably receive attention later on". Now that the table of tariffs had been agreed (in later minutes changes to the figures occur) it was agreed that the following figures should go forward to government:

Tomatoes.
April to July, three pence per pound.
August to March, two pence per pound.
December to March, one penny per pound.

Beans.
December to June, one shilling per pound.
July to November, three pence per pound.

Cucumbers.
March to June, twelve shillings per hundredweight.
July to October, eight shillings per hundredweight.

Grapes.
April to June, five pounds sterling per hundredweight.
July to October, three pounds sterling per hundredweight.

Mushrooms.
One shilling per pound all the year round.

After constructing the table of proposed tariffs within such a short time of Churchill's request for information and rapidly reaching agreement with all the other UK Glasshouse Associations on the figures that should be submitted, the Lea Valley Growers would no doubt have been disappointed with the any delays with regard to implementing the measures they had put forward. It is not clear from the minutes when the tariffs were implemented although we get occasional clues that something was probably in operation between 1932 and 1934. According to William Ashworth's *Economic History of England*, "An emergency tariff on non-essential imports was imposed in the autumn of 1931, and in 1932 the Import Duties Act established the framework of a permanent system".

The general election of November 1935 again saw the return of a National Government, now led by the Conservative Stanley Baldwin; Ramsey MacDonald having retired as Prime Minister earlier that year due to ill health. The Import Duties Act of 1932 had seen a general tariff of ten percent levied on all imports with the exception of some foodstuffs and raw materials. This figure was later increased to twenty percent and further increases followed. However, the government saw to it that preferential treatment was given to the old Empire and Commonwealth Countries.

Neville Chamberlain had been appointed Chancellor of the Exchequer in 1932, after the election of the National Government in 1931, the year that also saw Britain come off the gold standard. After the general election of 1935 Chamberlain was again appointed Chancellor. His approach to the tariff issue was to levy a ten percent tax on all foreign imports but this time, no doubt to the joy of the Lea Valley Growers, horticultural produce was included and as before the Empire and Commonwealth Countries were given favoured nations treatment. In the days before fast transport aircraft had arrived on the scene government ministers had probably concluded that the threat of competition from the far-flung countries of the Empire and Commonwealth to British growers was not an issue of immediate concern. The main threat to the Lea Valley Growers' profitability came from Europe and in particular the vast tomato industry of Holland which, through economy of scale, had the advantage of delivering cheap produce to the markets of Britain. It is also probable that the horticultural wholesalers in Britain were not too fussy where the produce came from as long as they could make an acceptable margin of profit.

THE 1930S

Throughout the 1930s and up until the beginning of the Second World War the minutes of the Association provide us with an insight into the day to day working of the Association and the concerns of the growers, which regularly had to be addressed, as they faced the impending crisis. This was normally done through a range of specialist sub-committees, although satisfactory solutions to the problems raised could not always be found. However, what is surprising is that the pre-war minutes, apart from the odd clue, are very much like any other Association minute and give very little away with regard to the build-up of international tensions.

The Council minutes for July 1931 record that Chivers & Sons, a famous firm of food manufacturers, had requested the growers to supply fifty tons of tomatoes for canning for which they were prepared to pay one shilling and three pence (about seven pence in today's money) for twelve pounds of the fruit. While this seems like a paltry amount it was probably looked upon by the growers as a way to sell tomatoes that would not have passed the market quality checks and also the arrangement would have been a good outlet for produce in times of seasonal glut. Unfortunately, after carrying out canning experiments the manufacturers concluded that they were unable to make a profit even if the cost of tomatoes was reduced to one shilling (five pence) for the twelve pounds.

In January 1932 the Association received a letter from Messrs Chapman Brothers who appear to have been interested in setting up a factory for the canning of fruit and vegetables. The enquiry was passed to the quaintly named Chutney Committee with a recommendation from the Council "for favourable consideration". From the lack of further information in the minutes it would seem that this initiative had also come to naught. One might speculate, had such initiatives been successful, the Lea Valley might have turned out to be a much different place today, with food canning plants operating alongside the glasshouse industry as the providers of produce, which would have made the region an important hub of food production. Opportunities such as this can change the course of history and it would appear that, in this particular case, history did not change, stopped in its tracks by something as small as a few pennies of cost.

For some time there had been concerns raised by growers who had nurseries in the Nazeing area regarding the activities of the local Hertfordshire and Essex Aeroplane Club. In August 1932, probably after a formal complaint from the growers, the Association received a letter from the club explaining that all their machines were insured to the tune of £5,000 against third party risks. While the communication seems to have gone some way to alleviating the Nazeing growers' fears, the Association's secretary reported that the Essex County Farmers' Union were asking the headquarters of the NFU to press for legislation to make it compulsory for all airmen to insure against third party risk.

It has been estimated that the Lea Valley was formed 1,000,000 to 1,800,000 years ago during the four glaciations (ice ages) of the Pleistocene Epoch. The last ice sheet, which geologists have estimated advanced from the north to a line across Britain that extended west-east from South Wales to South Essex, retreated approximately 10,000 years ago. During this departure, as the ice melted, the melt waters caused deposits of sand, gravel and clay to be brought down and it was these that formed the flood plain of the lower Lea Valley. The loamy conditions that developed made the region ideal for growing which later attracted the glasshouse industry to establish in the area.

Evidence of nature reclaiming an area where gravel was extracted at Cheshunt.

However, the enormous gravel deposits also made the region attractive to extraction companies as this valuable material is used on an industrial scale in the construction of roads, buildings and also in countless other civil engineering projects. As one might imagine the use of two quite different material resources, loam and gravel, by two quite different industries was often a source of conflict between the growers and the gravel extractors. Interestingly, the gravel extraction companies tend only to spend a short time in one location, usually until all the useful sand and gravel deposits are removed. The evidence of their operations can be seen all along the Lea Valley floor in a series of tell-tale pits which, after a time, can appear to the untrained eye as though they were natural features. Water from rainfall and from the aquifer gradually fill these pits giving nature the opportunity to take over, attracting a wide variety of birds, plants and other wildlife and in a relatively short time the ugly scars of the gravel extraction process vanish.

In January 1933 the Association received complaints from a nursery in the Broxbourne area that the Broxbourne Sand and Ballast Pits had "erected a screen" which was allegedly causing vibrations to occur in nearby glasshouses. The reference to a "screen" is probably to a power-driven mechanical device used in the grading of different sizes of ballast. In some cases a mechanical crusher is employed to break up large stones and boulders before the grading process and this machinery can be quite noisy in its operation. It would appear that the Council of the Association had difficulty in knowing how to deal with the alleged vibration problem and it was resolved to refer the matter to the NFU. However, nothing is seen in the minutes until March 1934 when a sub-committee of the Association paid a visit to the complaining Broxbourne nursery. After checking the various structures they reported that they were "unable to see any damage which it could say was directly attributed to the vibration; nor could the committee add to this report in regard to whether the vibration would damage the structure or shorten the life of the glasshouses as time proceeded". This seems to be a case of the grower in question being a little over anxious as to the long-term fate of his investment, or it is possible that he might have reasoned that having such an obtrusive operation in close proximity to his nursery could, in future, reduced the value of the business should he wish to sell.

The next reference to alleged problems which were thought to have been caused by a gravel extraction company occurs in April 1935. Growers in the Nazeing area complained to the Association that the pumping of water by the St. Albans Sand and Gravel Company had lowered the level of water in the nursery wells. An approach by the Association to the Ministry of Agriculture and also to the Ministry of Health to ascertain the legal position regarding the growers' loss of water was made. After deliberation by the ministries the Association received correspondence explaining that neither body was able to offer any help. Similar situations between the gravel extractors and the growers occurred in later years and these were never resolved satisfactorily.

At the Council meeting of July 1935 the secretary read out a copy letter from the Wessex Branch to the headquarters of the NFU that requested the Association's support in trying to close a possible loophole in the proposed system of tariffs. Wessex Branch had spotted that the government were in the process of examining certain tariffs and felt that while "specific duties on certain imported fruit pulp and canned fruit was under consideration, tomatoes should not be left out of the list". This was something that could have easily been missed when government framed future legislation and the meeting readily agreed to support the proposal.

At the same Council meeting the thorny question of tariffs arose again when a further letter was received from the headquarters of the NFU stating that the Working Branch had proposed a revision of the tomato duties. Their recommendation was as follows:

1st May to 30th June, three pence per pound.
1st July to 30th September two pence per pound.

The response by Council members to the suggestion was swift and to the point as the meeting resolved to write to NFU headquarters, "that this Council believes in a "shut-out" tariff from mid May to mid November provided that the interests of the Home Country are not prejudiced for the benefit of the Channel Islands".

After such a protectionist stance on tariffs there is a hint in the September 1935 Council minutes that some growers were prepared to operate double standards, particularly if the financial losses were to be borne by another industry. In this instance the Council received a letter from a grower who was complaining about the increase in the price of British horticultural glass and suggesting that the "matter being taken up with the government with a view to the tariff on foreign glass being removed". The meeting considered the member's suggestion and after they had compared glass prices with those in existence before "England left the Gold Standard and those in existence in 1932, after a 15 percent tariff had been placed on foreign glass", came to the conclusion that a case could not be made.

Tariff topics regarding horticultural produce feature frequently in the minutes of the Association. The Lea Valley Growers had, by the mid 1930s, become an established and respected part of a national growers network and had come a long way in a relatively short time since their beginnings in 1911. Through this network of growers they had ready access to government ministers and to other important people and organisations which allowed them the ability to flex their muscles collectively when lobbing on tariff and other issues. The Association had also discovered slightly more subtle ways to lobby through, what had become, the grand occasion of the annual dinner. Meeting minutes record that government ministers and other prominent people were regularly invited to these events which tended to be held in up-market London hotels and one might imagine the odd word being whispered in an influential ear over the after-dinner brandy and coffee!

In October 1935 a Special Committee consisting of Joseph Rochford, C H Shoults, J Harnett, Dr Bewley (of the Turners Hill Experimental Station) and also the Association's secretary was set up to look into a serious matter raised at the September Council meeting. Here a report had been presented by two members regarding a visit to "certain markets" and they were clearly concerned by the "appearance etc. of Lea Valley produce". The special meeting discussed the matter then drew up the following report to be presented to the Council:

It is evident that Lea Valley produce has lost its previous reputation in the markets of the Country. The situation is serious and must receive the considered and full attention of the Lea Valley Growers. The Committee realise that every care must be taken to prevent the present state of affairs from becoming public. It suggests that the first step should be a meeting of members only, at which Dr Bewley could explain the position and make suggestions which it is hoped, if carried out, will restore Lea Valley produce to its rightful position. With this end in view, the Committee suggests that a meeting be held at Walnut Tree House, on Monday, October 28th at 3 pm; with the President in the Chair and Dr Bewley as the speaker.

As a result of the recommendations of the Special Committee Dr Bewley addressed a meeting of members in November and explained that it had been proposed that lectures would be held for the growers, probably two on the subject of cultivation and one on picking, packing and marketing and, as it was customary, these recommendations went before the next Council meeting which duly endorsed them.

It seems rather odd that it was felt necessary to give the Lea Valley Growers, who were by now an established and respected national group of horticulturalists, a series of lectures on the basics of their profession. Such action would suggest that the growers had generally become complacent in their methods of growing, packaging and distribution and had allowed their standard of service to their customers to slip. If this was the case it would mean that the growers' long-term customer base would be bound to suffer and once this happened, as any supplier of goods and services will testify, it is then an up-hill, if not impossible, struggle to win back those lost or disappointed customers. If this were the case then the growers' actions would seem foolhardy in the extreme, particularly considering the strong and continuing competition coming from the nurseries abroad.

However, perhaps it was not all quite the fault of the growers. In an earlier minute it was discovered that, by way of a small-scale experiment, produce had been shipped to the northern markets by lorry as an alternative to the railway network. Here it is recorded that the produce arrived relatively quickly and in good condition and in a better state than if it had travelled by rail. As this experiment seems not to have been followed up by larger shipments of produce by road, could it be that the Lea Valley Growers were merely attempting to build up a pool of evidence that could be used in future negotiations with the railway company who had the monopoly on the bulk movement of horticultural produce?

It is probably no coincidence that in the Council minutes of May 1936 it is reported that the railway company have "despatched a ventilated railway wagon to Cheshunt for experimental purposes". Shipping produce in these modified wagons proved to be successful in maintaining the quality of the produce and later minutes of the Association show that the railway company despatched several more ventilated wagons for the growers' use, which further confirms the success of the project.

So with the wisdom of hindsight, the episode of produce arriving at the markets in poor condition had hopefully acted as a wake-up call to the growers and this particular chapter in their development had resulted from several contributory factors that should be shared between both the growers and the railway company. However, this serious incident should act as an example and be a salutary reminder to us all; as mentioned earlier, "When you begin to believe that your business is most successful, that is when your business is most vulnerable".

The Council meeting of November 1935 began in a rather unusual way when the chairman announced, before proceeding with the ordinary business, "that Mr H O Larsen's nursery had been purchased by Messrs Joseph Rochford & Sons Ltd". He then went on to express the view "that he felt certain the Council would be pleased that this nursery had fallen into such good hands". The minutes record that "the news was received with acclamation".

Mr H O Larsen, who died in July 1934, was a nursery

owner with a business at Waltham Abbey, Essex. Up until his death he had been continuously elected president of the Lea Valley Growers' Association since its founding in 1911. Throughout his membership Mr Larsen appears to have given more than his fair share of time to the running and development of the Association, his name appearing on a host of different working committees and he was also the instigator of many important initiatives within the horticultural industry.

After leaving a suitable period of time, out of respect for Mr Larsen's passing, Joseph P Rochford was unanimously elected president at the Association's Annual General Meeting in December 1934. Like his predecessor Mr Rochford was a founding member of the Association and also like his predecessor he worked tirelessly on many committees; his views and advice on an extraordinary range of horticultural and other subjects was always sought and enthusiastically welcomed by the Association's members. It is probably fair to say that Joseph Patrick Rochford (not to be confused with his late father Joseph Rochford (1856–1932) was part of the most famous dynasty of Lea Valley growers whose contribution to the horticultural industry in Britain and across the world is immeasurable.

The first time we get a hint of the coming war is in the Council minutes of January 1937 when it is reported that a letter had been received from the Cheshunt Urban District Council alluding to "air raid precautions". There is also a reference that information is also required as to the "number of motor vehicles which might be available to support the ambulance and or transport services". The meeting agreed to circulate members for information and also to defer further discussion until the next meeting. At around this time we note an increase in the level of complaints from growers over the "loss of workers to local factories". The main culprits in the theft of labour were the Royal Gunpowder Mills at Waltham Abbey and the Royal Small Arms Factory at Enfield Lock. This would tend to suggest that Britain was serious about the impending threat from Germany and was beginning to ramp up military production in preparation. In the face of the loss of skilled labour, the secretary was instructed to write to the headquarters of the National Farmers' Union "to see if anything could be done". This would appear to be a gesture on behalf of the Association to try and placate its membership as it was probably well accepted there was little that anyone could do to stop this haemorrhaging of labour while the country prepared for war.

The April Council meeting discussed the forthcoming

Coronation of George VI that would be held on 12th May and recommended that members should "give a holiday as far as possible in exactly the same way as was given at the Silver Jubilee". This equated to a day's holiday with pay and if it was necessary for employees to work it was further recommended that they should be, "paid in addition for the hours worked". In the early part of the twentieth century British people collectively shared a greater sense of patriotism than people today and an event such as the Coronation was to be celebrated with parties and family outings right across the country. It was probably the effects of this infectious patriotic mood that was sweeping the country which encouraged the growers to be a little more generous towards their workers.

British postage stamp to commemorate the coronation of King George VI, 1937.

At a time of national celebrations and with Britain bracing herself for war, one would have expected a growing harmonious working relationship between the growers and their workforce. However, the minute books contain a quite different story and record details of a Special Council Meeting that was called to address a single issue that clearly exposes a continuing atmosphere of unease that was surrounding the Lea Valley Growers' Association and the official nursery workers' representatives; the National Union of Agriculture Workers. To gain a feeling for the level of animosity that existed the opportunity has been taken to reproduce, below, the full text of a letter from the Lea Valley Growers' Association to the General Secretary of the National Union of Agricultural Workers, dated 7th May 1937:

Dear Sir,
Your letter of the 27th ult., addressed to the Lea Valley Growers' Association, was considered at a meeting of the Committee of this Branch of the National Farmers' Union yesterday, the 6th inst.
My committee expressed their surprise at your suggestions in regard to wage rates and would venture to point out that Statutory Agricultural Rates of Wages are already in force within the area covered by this Branch. The actual wages paid by employers engaged in glasshouse production are in most cases quite considerably in excess of the rates laid down by the Essex, Herts. and Middlesex Agricultural Wages Committees.
With reference to your remarks re lavatory,

mess-room and washing facilities, my committee cannot for a moment agree that the facilities provided are unsatisfactory. If you know of any specific cases which perchance you have in mind where these arrangements are not satisfactory I am instructed to say that if you put me in the possession of the necessary information I should be pleased to write to the employer/s in question suggesting some improvement, or alternatively, the matter could be submitted to the appropriate Wages Committee.

It is regretted that my Committee fail to appreciate that the subject matters of your letter are of such a nature as to be described as "urgent".

Yours faithfully,
(sgd.) F H Fullom

As the warm glow of togetherness that had enveloped Britain during the May Coronation was fading away, the growers at the June Council meeting were asked to consider a letter that had been received from the headquarters of the National Farmers' Union. After the meeting discussed the content the secretary was instructed to reply that "this Association is not in favour of extending the provision of holidays with pay compulsorily by legislation".

The July Council minutes show no warming of the Association's frosty relationship with the National Union of Agricultural Workers, in fact the situation could be described as worsening. It was reported by a Captain C G Reed, the secretary of the Hertfordshire branch of the NFU, that he recently had "informal conversations with the secretary of the Workers Union" who had wanted to establish "a Conciliation Committee". Captain Reed "hoped that a small Sub-Committee [of the Association] would be appointed to meet a special Committee from the men's Union, at which meeting the members appointed could make it perfectly clear that they were not prepared to attempt conciliation machinery". Without hesitation, the Council members resolved "not to meet the representatives of the Union, and that the following letter be sent":

Your letter WH/DJ of the 9th inst. was freely discussed by my Council at its meeting held yesterday, and after due consideration it was decided that no good purpose would be served by a meeting such as you suggest.

The minutes go quiet on the subject for six months until the February Council meeting of 1938 when the secretary is asked to reply to a letter from the National Union of Agricultural Workers. Although the content of the letter is not revealed, the tone of the following short reply leaves little to the imagination.

Your letter WH/KC of the 11th January was very carefully considered by my Council at its meeting yesterday. I am instructed to say that my Council regrets that it has nothing to add to its communication to you of the 15th of July last.

From the perspective of a twenty-first century outsider looking in it would seem that the Lea Valley Growers' Association had missed, once again, a golden opportunity to address a burning problem that was affecting all their members; the reasons why skilled nurserymen were leaving the industry to seek work in the nearby factories. While the Association was no doubt aware that the government factories, in particular, could offer better terms and conditions than the growers, one does suspect that there was something other than just wages and hours that were causing many workers to leave horticulture. After all, what had the growers to lose? They could have sat down with the workers representatives and found out the reasons for the unrest within their industry and, if they did not like what they heard or felt that they were unable to put things right, they could have then returned to their arms-length stance once more.

Breaking away from the subject of industrial relations it makes a refreshing and rewarding change, when following the progress of the Lea Valley Growers through the minute books of the Association, to discover a little known historical gem that connects one Lea Valley industry with another. In this particular instance the connection is made between two quite different industries, one that can trace its roots back hundreds of years, and the other which is a new embryonic technological industry that has its birthplace in the region. The world's first public service (high definition) television broadcasts began at 3p.m., on Saturday 2nd November 1936 from the mast of the BBC transmitter that was located at Alexandra Palace, Wood Green. The building and mast remains a London icon, silhouetted against the skyline on the crest of the ridge of the Lea Valley's western slopes.

The Council minutes for 10 November 1937 record "the secretary reported that the decorated vehicle so kindly supplied by Mr J C Randall had appeared in the Lord Mayor's Procession and created considerable interest. It had been reported in full by the BBC commentator, and had been televised". What is so remarkable about this event is that it would have been one of the earliest televised outside broadcasts, taking place only one year after the television service began and only six months

Alexandra Palace television mast would have broadcast the pictures, in 1937, of the Lea Valley growers float at the Lord Mayor's Show.

The crowd wait in anticipation for the Lord Mayor's procession. In 1937 BBC TV filmed the Lea Valley growers' float

after the Coronation of King George VI, which is claimed to have been the world's first high definition outside broadcast. Only a handful of people, in the London area, who possessed television receivers, were capable of viewing the event.

In the first few months of 1938 the minutes contain a number of references to a "Tomato Advertising Scheme" and although we are denied the details it is apparent that the Glasshouse Sub-Committee had been dealing with this project for some considerable time. Mr Bernard Rochford had been dispatched to the Channel Islands on behalf of the Association to invite the growers of Jersey and Guernsey to join the scheme. However, the Channel Island growers had delayed making a decision and Mr Rochford, because of time constrains in the implementation of the scheme, had to explain to the April Council meeting that after discussions with the headquarters of the National Farmers' Union the scheme would now proceed, "without the Channel Islands and that English tomatoes would be advertised". Scottish growers had also been invited to join the advertising scheme but had declined. This is probably why Mr Rochford talks about advertising "English" tomatoes rather than British.

As the prospect of war in Europe drew nearer there is a corresponding increase in the number of references to actions and preparations in the minutes as Britain braced itself for the coming conflict. The Hertfordshire secretary of the National Farmers' Union Branch had put out a circular after being approached by the War Office and the Air Ministry over the "taking of agricultural land for military purposes". Land would have been needed for the building of airfields, military camps, supply and storage depots, antiaircraft gun emplacements, searchlight batteries, radar and communication installations and prison camps to accommodate captured military personnel. At the time of the circular, none of the Lea Valley growers had been affected by these government demands. This was probably due to the growers' food production capability which would be crucial to Britain in wartime, so they were generally left alone.

The secretary raised the question of air raid precautions at the April Council meeting and the members resolved to form a special sub-committee. It was agreed that the committee would "consider and report to the Council whether suggestions should be made to members as to the protection of their workers in the event of an emergency".

At the May Council meeting a discussion ensued as to whether the government should be approached to ascertain their position with regard to the "likely damage to glasshouse property in the event of war". The secretary reported that he had been in touch with Mr Bernard Rochford, who was chairman of the Glasshouse Sub-Committee, and then proceeded to read a letter from Mr Rochford on the subject. The meeting then resolved to let Mr Rochford "bring the matter before the Glasshouse Sub-Committee, rather than submit a resolution from the Branch".

A copy of the government's *National Service* booklet had been received by the Association and the question of the schedule of reserved occupations was debated at the Council meeting held in February 1939. The meeting agreed to ask the headquarters of the National Farmers' Union their opinion as to whether, under the heading of Agriculture and Horticulture, they were "satisfied that the glasshouse workers came within any of the sub-headings mentioned, and if not make necessary application that they be so included". This would seem to be a clear indication that the Association was becoming concerned about the potential loss of skilled workers due to military conscription.

Also in the February Council minutes we see a reference, for the first time, to the Women's Land Army (WLA). In 1915, during the First World War, this body had been set up to take over the agricultural jobs of men who had been called up for service with the armed forces. After the war, as the men returned, the body was disbanded. The *National Service* booklet had mentioned that the WLA (set up for the second time in June 1939) would be employed on farm work. Therefore, the secretary was asked to contact the headquarters of the National Farmers' Union to "satisfy itself that the Army would be available for glasshouse work".

Another issue raised at the February Council meeting was the question of war risks insurance. After discussion the meeting decided to "leave the matter until such time as the government introduced its proposed Bill on the matter".

In the March Council minutes it was reported that Mr Bernard Rochford had been in touch with the Commissioner of Horticulture and he, "had been advised that glasshouse workers would come within the Schedule of Reserved Occupations". A reply had been received from the headquarters of the National Farmers' Union, in response to the Association's question regarding employment possibilities for the WLA. The communication explained that the NFU "had requested that this Body include the glasshouse industry in its activities". It is therefore assumed that the NFU were trying to clarify the matter with the appropriate government department.

The April Council minutes contain an amusing account of a member who had been served with an injunction over the use of his nursery siren and had taken his problem to the Association. Presumably he had used this device as an audible clock to alert workers to the starting and finishing times at his nursery. The Council discussed the member's complaint and concluded that, "this matter did not raise any question of principle affecting growers generally, and in the circumstances the Association could not incur any expenditure in defending the proceedings". I would guess that the injunction was taken out against the grower for repeated use of his siren after several warnings, as he had probably not complied with an initial request to silence the device. In the preparation for war

this request would have been perfectly reasonable as the authorities would not have wished the public to have become confused between the sounding of the growers and other official devices used to warn the community of an approaching enemy air raid.

By the May Council meeting the secretary had received a copy of the Military Training Bill and had pointed out to members that there was the possibility, under Section one, to adapt the training period to fit in with the growing season. The meeting resolved that a letter be sent to the headquarters of the National Farmers' Union, explaining that "the date for the glasshouse workers be put forward to October the 1st, but at the same time pointing out we had no wish to evade our obligations". As one might imagine Parliament was enacting a considerable amount of legislation in preparation for war as the aggressive expansionist policies of Germany made war with that country almost inevitable. On 26 May 1939, the Military Training Act was passed which meant that men between the ages of twenty and twenty-one were liable for six months military training, after which they would be transferred to the Reserve. However, at the outbreak of war, in September 1939, the Act was suspended when the National Service (Armed Forces) Act came into force.

In 1939, while all the preparations for war had been going on, the Association negotiated the purchase and had finally bought new offices at 126 Crossbrook Street, Waltham Cross, for £3,100, a very modest sum in comparison with today's property prices. The premises had formerly been the offices of the Cheshunt Building Society who were relocating to a nearby property in the same street. Previously the Association had rented offices at Bank Corner, Turner's Hill, Cheshunt.

Once all the contractual details had been completed a committee was appointed to consult with the Nursery Trades Ltd regarding their new tenancy. It was later agreed that the Nursery Trades Ltd should pay a rent of £40 per annum and that the secretary should pay an annual rent of £30. These combined annual rents equated to the amount paid by the Association to refurbish the whole building, including the secretary's accommodation, before anyone had moved in. The secretary being charged a rent would suggest that, at the time, it was customary for the secretary to live on the job.

The Prime Minister Neville Chamberlain declares war on Germany, September 1939.

Chamberlain returning from Germany in 1938 with the message, peace for our time.

THE SECOND WORLD WAR

Surprisingly the Council minutes of 13th September 1939, ten days after Britain and France declared war on Germany, are void of any discussion regarding the start of this world-changing event. At this meeting there were questions raised over whether workers should be paid due to "absence from work through air raids", and the members finally resolved that this was a matter for each individual nursery. The secretary read a letter from the Air Ministry with regard to the camouflaging of glasshouses and although the content of the communication is not known it was reported that the Council were in "full agreement". When the question of glasshouse camouflage had been raised some months earlier the growers had concluded that such an exercise was not practical. Interestingly, at the October Council meeting Mr Bernard Rochford reported on the subject of the camouflaging of glasshouses and stated that the "industry would hear no more of it".

Winston Churchill, who became Prime Minister in 1940, examines a Thompson light machine gun.

In the light of the various wartime restrictions quite a lot of the Association's business revolved around how to accommodate the authorities while at the same time maintaining an efficient and productive horticultural industry. In general there appears to have been a spirit of co-operation and compromise amongst the growers which is illustrated when the secretary reported, at the October Council meeting, that a number of members had been affected by the "calling up of workers under the age of 25" and he asked the meeting if anything could be done. Prior to the war, members were inclined to challenge most imposed decisions from official bodies but on this occasion their response was quite muted as it was agreed that, "no action should be taken".

Mr P J Butterfield, the chairman of the Council, reported that he had obtained police authority to carry out the steam sterilisation of glasshouses by a "method he had adopted of screening the lights". This initiative

was to comply with wartime black-out regulations that had been put in place to reduce the risk, in built-up areas, of night-time bombing raids by enemy aircraft. Similar precautions were taken to reduce the amount of tell-tale glow from glasshouse boiler grates when stoking was being carried out.

The October Council minutes, although lacking in specific detail, contain several references which indicate that the growers had to reorganise and prepare themselves for what might lie ahead. In many ways the Lea Valley horticultural industry had an advantage over many others as several of their active Council members were in place at the start of World War One and had a good idea of what would be required of them. When considering the question of War Risks Insurance it was Mr Bernard Rochford who took the lead in guiding members. At the time the National Farmers' Union had set up the National Farmers' Union Mutual Insurance Society Limited which had agreed to settle claims yearly, while other mutual bodies were withholding payments until after the war. After members had considered these schemes Mr Rochford "suggested a scheme which he had prepared" and although we do not know the details he did state that he thought it "was workable in the same way as Hailstone Insurance and it would cost approximately £25 per acre". The meeting agreed unanimously that the scheme "submitted by Mr Bernard Rochford was preferable". A committee was then elected to "consider, and if thought necessary, in conjunction with other glasshouse districts, to launch a scheme on the lines indicated by Mr Rochford".

We learn from the minutes that three county War Agricultural Committees had been set up covering the Lea Valley regions of Essex, Hertfordshire and Middlesex. While the minutes do not make the terms of reference, or the powers, of these committees clear there is a hint that they may be able to enforce certain conditions on Lea Valley nurseries. If this is the case the outcomes could be interesting as I note that a few members of the Association have been invited to sit on these committees!

At the same time as the county committees were being set up the Association had received a recommendation from the Minister of Agriculture with regard to the growing of carnations. Although we are not privy to the recommendation contained within the letter, it would have probably been something to do with reducing the production of flowers and increasing the growing of edible crops which, under the circumstances, would have been a normal wartime requirement. To help those growers who had only been involved with the cultivation of flowers and shrubs, the know-how of the Experimental Station was sought to provide advice on the growing of edible crops.

The meeting resolved to circulate the Minister's recommendation to members "with a note to the effect that these recommendations could be enforced by the County War Agricultural Committee". This might suggest that despite having the odd Lea Valley grower sitting on this or an appropriate sub-committee, the body could have been given some formal powers.

In the run-up to the war the government had tried to encourage growers to plough up or declare spare land within their nurseries for growing extra wartime crops but the growers had always appeared reluctant to become involved in such schemes. When the Association's secretary drew members' attention, at the October meeting, to land which they owned adjoining their glasshouses and asked "whether it was thought desirable to make any suggestions to the County Committee", their immediate response was, "to take no action". Keeping a low profile in these situations seems to have been very much the order of the day.

Within the first few weeks of the start of the war, a pattern was already beginning to emerge of increasing costs. Coal suppliers had been in contact with the Association suggesting that prices were due to rise. The coal companies also pointed out that the railway wagons had been taken over by the government and "an additional charge would arise". As wartime rationing of fuel came in, growers who had used more than one hundred tons of coal per annum by 30th June 1939, for heating their glasshouses and other nursery purposes, were told that they would not have to register with suppliers, but those who were using less would have to do so. As the horticultural industry had become an integral part of feeding Britain the growers would get the necessary supply of petrol and oil for those of their vehicles, which had not been commandeered by the authorities for other purposes, and also for their stationary nursery engines.

Further costs were soon to be incurred by the growers as the manufacturers of the tomato and cucumber boxes informed them that their prices were about to rise. Up until the war these boxes had been made of wood, soon to become a scarce wartime material, which gave the produce good protection during transit. Now that cardboard packaging was to be used this could increase the risk of produce being damaged. The growers appear resigned to the inevitability of having to absorb any rise in the cost of packaging as they agreed "that no purpose would be served in objecting to the increase".

One of the last entries in the minutes relates to a letter sent to a grower by a Covent Garden salesman and read by the secretary to the meeting, the content of which could pose serious problems for all growers. It would seem that an arrangement existed where the Covent Garden salesmen would support individual growers by making an up-front payment to help finance and secure the next generation of produce. On this occasion the salesman had stated that "it was not possible to carry out the usual financing of growers in view of the great risk involved", of course he was referring to the war and the possible damage to glasshouses from air raids. These concerns had already been reported to the headquarters of the National Farmers Union and it was suggested that should this financial arrangement be lost then it could mean that "fifty to one hundred acres of glasshouses would possibly be standing empty". Bernard Rochford reported that the matter had been "mentioned already to the appropriate government department, and would be brought forward at a meeting to be held next Wednesday". Unfortunately we shall never know the outcome as we have reached the end of the minute book and there are no further minutes covering the period of the war.

While it is possible that no more minutes were written, I suspect that the minute books for this period have been lost. I say this because the minutes of 12th October 1939 were signed by the chairman, Mr P J Butterfield one month later on 9th November 1939. It is normal practice at each new meeting for the minutes of the previous meeting to be read by the secretary and the question is normally asked whether they are a correct record of the business which took place. This allows members the opportunity to raise corrections to the minutes. If the meeting then agrees that everything has been correctly recorded the chairman will sign the minutes to this effect. Therefore, it would seem logical to conclude that because the October minutes were signed one month after the meeting this would suggest that this was done at a time when the November Council meeting was taking place. This being the case, we would have expected to have seen the business of this meeting and the following wartime meetings recorded in a new minute book. As this item was not to be found within the Lea Valley Growers archive, one must conclude that the book had either been lost or destroyed.

The reader will recall that Bernard Rochford had proposed an improved insurance scheme for the growers to compensate them for losses or damage that they might sustain from enemy action during the war years. Ironically the first serious damage did not come from a raid by German aircraft, but from something much closer to home. On 18th January, 1940 there was a massive explosion at the Royal Gunpowder Mills at Waltham Abbey. The force of the blast was such that it shattered 62,453 panes of glass and caused other structural damage to a number of glasshouses in the region. The blast is recorded as happening at 10.42 in the morning and was so severe that not only were glasshouses damaged but windows in Waltham Abbey were blown in and the force of the explosion was felt, and heard, across London and the Home Counties. Even a seismograph at the Kew Observatory picked up the shock waves. Sadly five men working at the Royal Gunpowder Mills lost their lives and others were injured. The blast happened while three of these men were working in a nitro-glycerine mixing house, when six thousand pounds of the material exploded, setting off a severe chain reaction.

After the explosion, growers were forced to apply for special licences to obtain supplies of scarce timber to repair the damage to their glasshouses. It should be remembered that in these times of wartime austerity, government restrictions were in place and only essential repairs were being allowed.

The cost of the damage to the growers was estimated at over £4,600, a fairly substantial sum for the day. Therefore, one has to wonder whether the insurance scheme, proposed by Bernard Rochford, covered such eventualities as glasshouses being wrecked by a so called "friendly explosion". Unfortunately we shall probably never know the answer with regard to the financial outcome because of the loss of the Council minute books for the period. Interestingly a reference to the explosion was included in the booklet of the Golden Jubilee of the

A completely demolished nitro-glycerine mixing house at the Royal Gunpowder Mills where five men lost their lives, 18th January 1940.

Further devastation at the Royal Gunpowder Mills caused by the explosion on 18th January 1940.

Lea Valley Growers' Association as "damage caused by enemy action" on "18th January, 1948" and as the reader will appreciate this is clearly a mistake. Further research has confirmed that the earlier date of the explosion is correct and this makes it clear that the tragedy could not have been caused by "enemy action".

A stark reminder of the occupation of the Channel Islands. The occupation stopped the export of tomatoes to Britain during the Second World War.

Despite not having the later minutes to work from we do know of a number of wartime events which affected the Lea Valley horticultural industry which have been recorded in a range of books, newspapers and journal articles. For example we know that the Channel Islands were occupied by the German armed forces in June 1940 until the end of the War and this immediately put paid to the island's export of tomatoes to Britain. Just prior to the invasion Germany had sent reconnaissance aircraft over the islands to discover how they were being defended and the reports came back that there were troop concentrations on the Guernsey Docks. The news prompted the Luftwaffe to send aircraft to bomb the docks of both Guernsey and Jersey. However, as it happened, the reconnaissance turned out to be wrong as the German aircrews had mistakenly taken the trucks, which were lined up on the dockside, to be troop carriers when in fact they were waiting to unload tomatoes to be exported to Britain. Forty-four people were killed in the raids.

In May 1940, after the severe bombing of Rotterdam, the Netherlands were occupied by German military forces and the country remained under their control until liberated by Canadian troops in 1945. The Dutch growers had been one of the Lea Valley's major peacetime threats with their cheap exports of produce to the UK. Now with the Netherlands and Channel Islands under German occupation the British growers were gifted an unexpected bonus, albeit not in a gloating way, as they were free to increase their home production without fear of low prices or dumping from these sources of overseas competition.

Observation tower built by the German armed forces who occupied the Channel Islands during the Second World War.

Wartime ration book and coupons which ensured that each person received their fair share of food from the retailer.

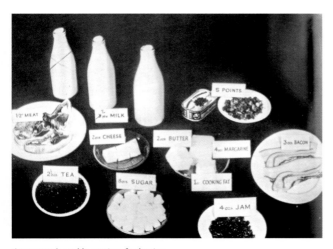

One person's weekly wartime food ration.

Early in the war, the German Navy had stepped up its U-boat campaign and also that of laying explosive mines in the seas around Britain which caused considerable losses to merchant shipping bringing food and other essential goods to this country. This increased the pressure on the agricultural and horticultural industries and encouraged growers, like those in the Lea Valley, to become more productive. To help ease the food supply crisis, the government launched a campaign called "Digging for Victory" where ordinary citizens were encouraged to grow their own vegetables in gardens, allotments and on spare pieces of land. Several people also began keeping rabbits, chickens and ducks to help supplement their rations of meat and eggs. Some shady entrepreneurs took advantage of the rationing system by obtaining supplies of scarce food and other supplies directly from farmers and elsewhere and sold it at elevated prices to wealthy clients. The system was known as the "black market" and was, of course, illegal. There were others who saw an opportunity in another illegal enterprise, that of poaching, taking game at night from the large country estates and selling it on. Those shady characters were involved in these illegal entrepreneurial enterprises were commonly known as "Spivs". These unscrupulous people lived by their wits, taking advantage of the shortages created by the wartime rationing, while trying not to get caught by the police in the process.

Early in 1940 food rationing, through a system of ration books with coupons, was introduced and customers had to register with a particular butcher and a grocer. Once registered, the customer would have to stay with these outlets which would then be allocated the appropriate quantities of food which could then be distributed fairly. Everyday products like bacon, ham, meat, butter, margarine, cheese, cooking fats, milk, sugar, sweets, preservatives, breakfast cereals, biscuits, eggs as well as canned fruits, fish and meats were strictly limited. However, some other products, for a whole range of reasons, could be in short supply and would be restricted to the grocer, who might be tempted to save some "below the counter" for his favourite customers. As the war progressed, more products were included in the rationing system like fuels, soap and clothes. Before the war Britain imported around twenty million tons of its foodstuffs per year; this figure fell soon after the commencement of hostilities by around seventy percent.

In times of hardship even established bodies can become quite inventive. The BBC, for example, launched radio programmes like "Kitchen Front", which suggested simple, quick and easy recipes for pies and puddings and other dishes by using a variety of easily available vegetables. Some of these dishes were specifically created, to include textures and flavours that substituted the original ingredients, to trick the palate into thinking that it was consuming the traditional dish. Of course this was not always successful. Also there was the radio gardener, C H Middleton, who dispensed tips on how and when to grow vegetables, through his weekly programme, In *Your Garden*. Middleton also published at least two successful books that were based on the programme which were widely read, particularly by those who had never been required to pick up a spade before.

The late Peter Rooke (1927–2007) allows us a glimpse of the Lea Valley nursery industry through his book *Cheshunt at War* when he explains the effects of government regulations on the growing of non-essential foods. As someone who lived in the area with family and other connections to the nurseries Peter was able to narrate how the Rochfords had to grub out their mature grape vines and how Stevens, a prominent grower of

A wartime poster encouraging people to dig up gardens and waste land to grow vegetables.

flowers and shrubs, were forced to dig up their world-renowned rose bushes to make way for essential crops. Apparently a small amount of stock was allowed to be retained in anticipation of a post-war recovery.

Peter tells us that the growing of cucumbers was banned as they were considered to be of little nutritional value and their propagation was also responsible for consuming large amounts of scarce fuel for heating. Tomatoes became the preferred crop and wartime regulations made their marketing much simpler. No longer had the growers to abide by the peacetime grading of fruit by size and quality; all they were required to do was to collect together tomatoes of all shapes and sizes and weigh them into twelve-pound boxes then despatch them to market. There was also an added bonus for the growers who were now in receipt of government controlled prices for their produce the sale of which was effectively guaranteed.

Although nursery workers came under the "reserved occupation" regulations this did not stop many volunteering for military service or opting to work in the factories within the region. Many of these factories had changed their production from peacetime goods to manufacturing products essential to the war effort and were now under government control. The shortage of labour within the horticultural industry brought elderly men out of retirement and women were also encouraged to take up seasonal employment. Peter Rooke tells us that later in the war Italian prisoners of war were employed and shortly afterwards German prisoners too. Lorries were sent to a prisoner of war camp each day, located at Newgate Street near Cuffley, and men were taken to their respective nurseries and put to work. While Peter mentions that "some nurseries employed Land Girls" it is difficult to gauge how widespread this practice was throughout the Lea Valley horticultural industry.

In an article in *Hertfordshire Past*, issue 42, Peter writes about the damage to many glasshouses in the Cheshunt area caused by enemy raids. He cites an unnamed nursery in Andrews Lane, Cheshunt that was struck by a string of bombs that caused the whole tomato crop to be discarded because of the risk of glass splinters in the fruit. On another occasion he mentions a nursery in Cheshunt that was completely wrecked when a landmine exploded in the air above it. Glasshouses, being constructed of fragile materials, were also vulnerable to the vibrations and shock waves from the gun batteries in the vicinity as they tried to engage the enemy raiders.

Compared with the First World War, growers who endured the Second World War would have suffered greater disruptions to their businesses and also increased structural damage to their glasshouses as the technology of warfare had become much more sophisticated. Air raids were now more frequent and the bombs dropped by the Luftwaffe were packed with larger amounts of improved explosives that were more deadly and destructive than those crude devices dropped by the Zeppelins and Gothas.

The war finally came to an end in Europe in May 1945, with the fall of Japan slightly later when the surrender documents were signed in September of that year.

Mr C H Middleton's wartime gardening book. Middleton was a popular wartime broadcaster giving tips on how to grow vegetables.

Women Land Army workers showing their newly acquired skills.

Women's Land Army poster (1939–1945).
This was designed to get women volunteering
to work in the agricultural and horticultural
industries.

THE IMMEDIATE POST-WAR PERIOD

As might be imagined it would take several years before Britain and the Lea Valley horticultural industry could return to normal and in fact normality, as judged by pre-war standards, would never return to the region. Not all men being demobilised from the armed forces returned to horticulture as many had learned new skills and it was these skills that were in high demand as Britain slowly got back on her feet. Returning servicemen, who had formerly worked in horticulture, had learned construction, electrical and mechanical engineering skills and these were some of the assets that were needed to re-build the country that had suffered considerable losses and damage to its roads, railways, docks, housing, utility supplies, manufacturing industries and the general service infrastructure.

In May 1945, almost immediately after the cessation of hostilities in Europe, a general election was called. Winston Churchill, who had led the coalition government during the war years, lost to his wartime deputy Clement Attlee who secured a surprise landslide victory for the Labour Party. The cost of the war had almost bankrupted the British economy and the incoming government was forced to sell off a considerable amount of its overseas investments to begin the task of paying off its wartime debts.

In an effort to rebuild Britain, an enormous challenge by any standards, the government took control, through a programme of nationalisation, of the Bank of England, the steel industry, the coal mines, the gas, water and electricity supply companies, civil aviation, the railways, road transport and the canals. Because of the lack and scarcity of materials needed for the rebuilding programme, the government kept in place several wartime restrictions to ensure fairness of supply. Even food rationing was maintained, not being fully phased out until July 1954. This was the scale of the austerity environment that surrounded the country, and the Lea Valley growers would have to get to grips with this if they wished to reconstruct their own industry.

Post-war Labour Party poster that helped to secure a landslide election victory in 1945.

Women ensure that the milk gets delivered during the great freeze of 1947.

Clement Attlee with King George VI after the surprise election result for the Labour Party in 1945.

As the new government struggled to rebuild Britain, while at the same time negotiating with her Allies over the reconstruction of Germany and the rest of Europe, in the winter of 1946–1947 the country experienced one of the worst cold spells in recorded history. Temperatures plummeted to below zero, deep snow blocked the roads and railways, villages were cut off and areas of sea around Britain froze. Precious supplies of coal could not be transported to the power stations and to other essential users and this resulted in further disruption of services accompanied by power cuts. The situation was made even worse as people rushed to the shops to buy up the few remaining electric fires to warm their freezing homes as domestic coal and coke stocks ran low and in some places completely ran out. This in turn increased pressure on the already creaking power supply industry and in an effort to cope the government limited power-consuming television broadcasts and also the production of news print.

Chaos in Trafalgar Square in the great freeze of 1947.

The scarce fuel situation would almost certainly have affected the Lea Valley growers as they relied heavily on regular supplies of coal and coke. These fuels were needed to ensure that steam sterilisation of glasshouse soil could take place along with the running of boilers that provided the heating for their large glasshouses and propagation facilities.

Food supplies in the shops became low as farmers were unable to get vegetables out of the frozen ground, livestock starved through lack of feed and thousands of cattle and sheep that had been caught in snowdrifts died. Members of the armed services were drafted in and given the job of helping to clear snow from the railways and roads. Ironically German prisoners of war, who had yet to be repatriated and were perhaps some of the men whom these British soldiers had helped capture, were also put to work alongside their old adversaries to clear the blocked railway lines.

When the thaw finally came, in March 1947, the country saw some of the worst flooding in its history. Tragically the thaw was accompanied by weeks of torrential rain which could not be absorbed by the frozen ground and the run-off, which found its way into the rivers and streams, caused many of the country's major waterways, including the River Lea, to burst their banks. Thousands of people were displaced and the emergency services were stretched to breaking point rescuing and re-housing the stranded.

One of the good things for the Lea Valley region, which came out of the flooding disaster, was the start of construction, in 1947, of the River Lee Flood Relief Channel. The scheme, finally completed in 1976, flows southward from Ware in Hertfordshire along the valley floor to meet with the City Mill River at Stratford in east London. From there the water flows into the Lee Navigation, joining the waterway south of Old Ford Lock. The government of the day must be congratulated for their courage in commissioning such an expensive and long-term scheme while Britain was in the grip of grave austerity measures. They were either extremely lucky or gifted with considerable foresight, as who could have predicted the severe environmental effects, caused by global warming, that our world is experiencing in the twenty first century? It is probably fair to conclude, that, if the flood relief channel had not been built, the current nurseries that straggle the Lea Valley floor would not have the same degree of environmental protection that they enjoy today.

Those Lea Valley growers who had endured the hardships of war, including bombing and explosions, and then navigated their businesses through the post-war harsh winter and the flooding must have thought that things could only get better. However, there were still a few surprises for the horticultural industry that were yet to be revealed.

Troops clearing railway tracks of snow during the harsh winter of 1947.

A train ploughs its way through the floods of 1947.

The confluence of the River Lea flood relief channel (in the foreground) with the River Lea. Picture taken just south of Enfield Island Village.

THE NEWS LETTERS OF THE LEA VALLEY GROWERS' ASSOCIATION BEGIN

From March 1948 a series of the Lea Valley Growers' Association News Letters exist and, although not complete this new source provides sufficient material to continue the story which could have abruptly ended with the loss of the minute books. The News Letter first began life as a short in-house produced information sheet and soon progressed to a multi-paged publication that was professionally printed. Over the years, the News Letters attracted several pages of advertisements from the various horticultural service providers which no doubt off-set the increased cost of production.

One of the first major debates of the post-war period concerned the marketing and distribution of tomatoes and these issues were discussed by both growers and government departments. The Lucas Committee had been set up to consider the working of the Agricultural Marketing Acts, 1931–1933, and another body named the Fruit and Vegetable Organisation, under the chairmanship of Dr Edith Summerskill, was given the task of investigating what improvements could be made to the marketing and distribution of fruit and vegetables. It seems that there were two sets of conflicting views of how the distribution and marketing of produce should be carried out.

One view suggested that the growers' control should end at the nursery or farm gate. A counter opinion thought that the growers should have overall control of the marketing and distribution of their produce. As one might expect the growers were in favour of the latter while the Lucas Committee were in favour of the former. This, the Committee had argued, was on the grounds that it was the job of the grower to produce the crop, while the marketing and distribution of the product should be left to the "experts". To counter this point of view, the growers put forward a quite powerful and cogent argument which suggests that they had done their homework. In this they claimed that they had observed, in just about every case of branded goods, for example, tobacco, motor cars, radio equipment and processed foods it is the producers that have control of those involved in the distribution of their products. They also argued that the producer fixed the price and the terms and conditions of sale and in many cases they observed that there was a direct link between the producer and the consumer through the issuing of product guarantees. It was further argued that the only way that produce, which was perishable, could be guaranteed to arrive in good condition at market, particularly after being passed through the growers centres that were now becoming involved in the packaging and grading of produce, could only come with the acceptance of the principle of "Producer Control".

From the May 1948 News Letter we discover, in a special communication from the Association's chairman, that "Producer Control", had come much closer to reality within a very short time. In the piece we learn that the government had recently published The Tomato Control Order for 1948 which had imposed a controlled price on tomatoes and also ended the statutory tomato distribution scheme. There appear to have been considerable negotiations carried out behind the scenes between the Association's Executive Committee led by Bernard Rochford and the Ministry of Food. Their hard

An early picture of Turnford Hall. This is where the Lea Valley growers met to rubber stamp The Tomato Control Order for 1948.

work and dedication received the almost unanimous backing from a special meeting of the growers convened at the Turnford Hall of Thomas Rochford and Sons. Now the Association was in a position to take control of the distribution of their tomatoes but they had to promise that the growers "would send no less than half [of their] tomatoes during the period of Price Control to Midland and Northern Markets in consultation with the Ministry". Although the scheme was voluntary it was pretty obvious that a large number of the growers were prepared to co-operate and make it work. The committee had also negotiated special terms with the rail authorities to transport their produce to the markets around the country in bulk.

To ensure that the transportation of goods flowed smoothly a separate company was set up, Lea Valley Growers'Transport Limited, which oddly enough did not have any vehicles. The idea was that growers who joined the company would be issued with share certificates and any profits made, after administration and other costs were taken into account, would be shared between members. Growers would be responsible for getting their produce to the railway stations at Broxbourne, Cheshunt and Waltham Cross where representatives would ensure that the individual grower's fruit would be loaded for the correct destinations and also these people would provide any other assistance. Now that the overall distribution arrangements, negotiated by Bernard Rochford and the Executive Committee were in place, along with the new transport facilities to ship produce out of the Lea Valley, this would suggest that the LVGA had establish themselves as a force to be reckoned with.

In January 1949, the Vice-chairman of the Association's executive committee, L C Madsen, had been invited to appear on the BBC radio series *Farming Today*. This was an opportunity not to be missed as it gave the Association a platform on which it could put forward their views on how marketing of produce should take place in a post-war atmosphere of austerity and strict government control and regulation.

As an example of how restrictive these post-war regulations could be, in 1948 an anonymous whistle blower had reported the Lea Valley Growers'Association to the Board of Trade for breaking an Order, regarding the amount of advertising material carried in their monthly newsletter. The existence of this Order was completely unknown to Association members. Under a Paper Control regulation, any publication which was not in existence before 1939 should not contain a certain percentage of advertising material and also the amount

of paper to produce each issue should not exceed a certain weight. While the Association's newsletter was well under the permitted weight limit the only way they were able to get round the problem, without upsetting their advertisers who were relied upon to fund the periodical, was to double the size of each month's issue from twenty to forty pages and then not to accept additional advertisements. Such crazy regulations made a complete mockery of the legislative process and resulted in the exact opposite outcome that the designers of the Order had hoped to achieve.

Mr Madsen's script for the programme allows us a unique insight into some interesting facts and also the thinking behind a marketing scheme that was intended to bring together, not just the nurseries and smallholdings within the Lea Valley region, but all the different categories of growers throughout the United Kingdom.

Madsen's script identifies the difficulties of marketing products as diverse as root vegetables, outside-grown fruit, vegetables and flowers, indoor-grown fruit, vegetables and flowers and salad crops, all of which have their different seasons. He points out that over the last fifty years "cucumbers have established a wide popularity as a salad vegetable" and "fresh tomatoes have become a necessary part of modern diet", stating that the annual crop is around 125,000 tons which he valued at about £15 million. It is clear that the radio programme was to be used to challenge the central control of government in how produce should be marketed. He also wanted to suggest how the UK growers could be brought together as a unified horticultural industry. The scheme being highlighted by Madsen had been some time in its creation and had already been proposed to government by the National Farmers' Union.

It would appear that a lot of thought had gone into the scheme and one can see that much of its construction had been influenced by practical experience learned over the years. There is no doubt that the Association was wishing to greatly improve the efficiency and quality of their marketing and distribution which suggests that they were planning for the long-term survival of their industry as they had recognised a once-in-a-lifetime opportunity to establish themselves as a serious supplier of the nation's food while the post-war austerity measures were still in place.

In essence the scheme was to establish a Marketing Board of thirty-four members, democratically elected by districts, covering the whole of England, Wales and Scotland. Initially it was intended that the Board should be regulatory with few powers of compulsion. However, included within the scheme was the provision for a further vote by growers, if the Board considered that producers should be asked for a mandate on the taking of compulsory powers with regard to buying, selling, grading and packing. These powers could only be implemented by a two-thirds majority vote. If the scheme came into force, all growers of tomatoes and cucumbers who had more than one-thirty-second of an acre under glass (five hundred tomato plants or one hundred cucumber plants), or one-sixteenth of an acre in the open (four hundred plants) would have to register with the Board if they wished to sell their produce. It would also be a requirement that registered growers would have to provide statistics of their production if asked to do so by the Board.

The Board's activities would be financed by a levy on growers that amounted to not more than fifteen shillings per unit (seventy-five pence in today's money), a unit being defined as one-thirty-second of an acre under glass or one-sixteenth of an acre in the open for tomatoes; cucumbers would be levied against the same acreage but the plants would be confined to one hundred. A further, and crucial, part of the scheme was for the Board to compile a register of approved salesmen. In the past the Association had experienced sharp practices by some sales personnel and they wanted to ensure that they only dealt with "salesmen whose integrity can be relied on who undertake to observe reasonable commission and handling rates". For the scheme to work members could only use approved salesmen and there would be financial penalties imposed by the Board for any transgressions by the growers after an appropriate investigation had first taken place. While some growers had raised the question that the latter looked like a "snoopers' clause" it was pointed out that the Board "consisted of the growers' representatives".

Also the March 1948 Association's News Letter contains a very interesting article that allows a unique insight into the labour shortages that were affecting Lea Valley growers. Apparently the Association had been advised by the Ministry of Labour that the "Galley Hill Camp at Waltham Abbey would be cleared of German prisoners and ready to receive the Poles by 8th March". As there were considerable labour shortages at nurseries in the Nazeing, Waltham Abbey, Sewardstone, Broxbourne and Cheshunt areas the government were trying to find a solution to this particular problem. The idea was to encourage former Polish military personnel to respond to a Ministry of Labour circular inviting them to apply to

Aircrew of the Polish 303 Squadron. It was servicemen like these who did not wish to return home after the Second World War that the Lea Valley nurseries wanted to recruit.

work at these nurseries. It is probable that these Polish soldiers had been fighting the Nazis and were unable, or unwilling, to return home because of the Russian takeover of Poland.

Growers were reminded by the Association that applications for individual Polish workers had to be made through the Waltham Abbey office as they wished to ensure that the men were employed in the nearest nurseries to the camp. It is therefore possible that with fuel supplies being short, the growers were trying to keep transport costs to an absolute minimum. The Galley Hill Camp was located east of the present B194 road a little to the east of Hayes Hill Farm. It would appear that the Ministry was using this initiative as a pilot scheme to attract 250 men to the area. If the project turned out to be successful, more camps would be set up in the region. It was thought by the Ministry that most men applying for the work would be ex-officers and those with "any type of growing experience" would be the first to be chosen. This does suggest that the local horticultural labour shortage was pretty desperate.

The British Army had been given the job of making the Galley Hill Camp ready to receive personnel by 8th March and furnish it to "hostel standards", a task they completed two days early. One month later the growers were complaining to the Ministry of Labour that the Polish workers had not yet arrived and rumours were circulating that German prisoners might be moved into the region until the Polish workers were available. Why the Polish workers had not arrived is unclear and from the various reports the scheme seemed to be descending into chaos. The Association was now advising its members that the "Ministry of Labour now ask if our growers in other districts will say how many permanent staff they require, in order that more Polish labour can be put into camps in the Cheshunt area, etc., and we now ask members to apply to this office".

Members were now being advised that they could obtain Displaced Persons or European Voluntary Workers at a minimum agricultural wage rate of one shilling and tenpence-halfpenny per hour (around nine pence in today's money) from their respective County Agricultural Committees if they were willing to sign a contract giving employment for at least three months. Should the growers take this option then they would have to accept responsibility for transporting the workers to and from the nurseries and their respective camps.

In the past individual growers had been accustomed to operating their businesses with the minimum of internal office administration and they were extremely protective about not letting anyone, particularly the agricultural workers' trade union, influence in any way the terms and conditions of their arrangements with their employees. This was regarded as very much the prerogative of the growers' particular business arrangements and they were strongly opposed to having any form of recognised

collective agreements across the horticultural industry. Now, with direct government input into their businesses, everything was about to change. In future growers would have to introduce, and strictly maintain, new administrative systems within their individual businesses which would allow government departments to monitor the activities of their respective workers.

In March 1948 the government announced that they were introducing the National Insurance Act and the National Insurance (Industrial Injuries) Act and the legislation, for these Acts, was scheduled to come into force on 5th July, 1948. The Acts were designed to apply to everyone in the country over school leaving age and there would be three classes of insured persons; Class I, employed persons, Class II, self-employed persons and Class III, non-employed persons. These two Acts were designed to cover benefits such as sickness, unemployment, maternity, pensions, widow's benefits, death grants and industrial injury benefits. The introduction of such major reforms, particularly for the smaller nurseries, would have no doubt caused anxieties within those businesses that were administratively not set up for the task and it is probable that the owners would have been faced with some serious decisions. These would have been along the lines; should we take on administrative staff and bite the legislative bullet, or should we get out of the horticultural business altogether?

Polish soldiers who fought with the British during the Second World War remained in Britain after the war and worked in the Lea Valley nursery industry.

THE 1950S

As Britain entered the new decade there was a growing feeling of optimism mingled with the sense of the mammoth task that still lay ahead to rebuild a war-torn nation. Food shortages remained in the shops with rationing restrictions still in place on certain foodstuffs. Essential building and stocks of necessary materials, needed by industry, had yet to get back to pre-war levels and in London and many towns and cities around Britain the scars left by the Luftwaffe were there for all to see. In the midst of all the post-war austerity and the need to get the country back on its feet, it might appear somewhat surprising to learn, particularly to an outsider, that the British government would contemplate, in May 1951, the launch of the Festival of Britain. This was a major purpose-built exhibition with the principal buildings centred on the south bank of London's River Thames where the Festival Hall, a building remaining from the period, stands today. Other events and festivities took place in towns and cities around Britain.

Part of a set of postage stamps to commemorate the Festival of Britain in 1951.

The purpose of the Festival was to celebrate the centenary of the Great Exhibition of 1851, held in the Crystal Palace, a massive glass-covered building, designed by Joseph Paxton and erected in London's Hyde Park. Apart from the 1951 Festival being staged to showcase Britain's engineering, technological and cultural achievements it was also designed to lift the nation out of the gloom left over from the war years and to point the way to a brighter settled future.

The Festival of Britain as seen from the River Thames with the Skylon and the shot tower showing up against the skyline.

The 1951 Festival of Britain, London's South Bank, to celebrate the start of a new beginning after World War Two. It was also to commemorate the centenary of the Great Exhibition in 1851.

During this period of the early 1950s Lea Valley Growers, like many other businesses and industries around Britain, had been caught up in the post-war austerity measures. In trying to rebuild their interests Lea Valley growers, as an industry, appear to have been dealt an uneven hand of cards. Apart from having to endure fuel shortages, power cuts and the lack of skilled labour, the situation was made even worse when the government began the process of closing the camps in the region that housed the former prisoners of war and displaced persons that were an essential source of the growers' labour.

Further problems were caused to the Lea Valley horticultural labour force when changes were made to the 1948 National Service Act. Initially the Act was designed to take fit men between the age of eighteen and twenty-one years into military service for a period of eighteen months. However, in response to the demands of the Korean War, in October 1950, the service period was extended to two years. In 1951 the net loss of labour in Essex alone was 1,500 employees representing five percent of the workforce. And, as if these problems were not enough for the growers to bear, they were having to become involved in fighting their corner at numerous public enquiries as different local authorities began issuing compulsory purchase orders to acquire prime nursery land for large-scale housing projects. These were planned to house the growing population of dormitory workers as the post-war push to expand and modernise old factories and to create new industries within the region became stronger.

A British Railways train passing glasshouses. The Lea Valley horticultural industry relied heavily on the railways for produce and coal deliveries.

However, with all these problems on their plate, the growers still found time and energy to send produce to the South Bank Exhibition to be displayed in the Country Pavilion. The records indicate that the following members submitted produce under the following range of categories:

Fern
Thomas Rochford & Sons Ltd.

Tomatoes
Joseph Rochford & Sons Ltd.
E G Fouracres & Sons Ltd
G & C D Chapman Ltd.
E F Meering Ltd.
L R Wilson & Sons.

Cucumbers
Haslemere Nurseries Ltd.
Joseph Rochford & Sons Ltd.
Chalk Field Nurseries Ltd.
L R Wilton & Sons.

Carnations
E G Fouracres & Sons Ltd.
Charles Madsen Ltd.

By 1952 there were further concerns for the growers regarding shortages of skilled labour as the government began issuing recall notices to all former servicemen, of Class "Z" Reservists status, for annual military training

for periods of fifteen days. This could prove severely disruptive to those nurseries already suffering skills shortages, particularly if men were called away during the peak season. After complaining to the authorities the growers were informed that all persons called for training must serve, "whatever their occupation" and only personal hardship or one-man businesses could be considered for appeal. One can gauge how critical labour shortages within the Lea Valley horticultural industry had become when the April 1952 News Letter floated the idea of setting up a thirteen-week residential training programme for young girls and boys between the ages of fifteen and seventeen. The proposed scheme was to be modelled on the Town Boys and Girls Scheme that had recently been set up to train young farm workers.

While reading the above News Letter I could not help but notice a short article that included an extract of a radio broadcast by E H Gardener, Chairman of the Central Horticultural Committee of the National Farmers' Union.

Gardener, in the article, makes the point that, "In the first place the increase in the bank rate and the increase in petrol and oil duties are going to add materially to our costs. A great many growers, as do the farmers, require an overdraft from their bank at certain times of the year so that they may finance the crops they grow. The last two lean years in the vegetable industry have meant that for some of us the overdraft is required all the year round. An increase in the bank rate is going to mean a substantial increase in the rates which will be charged on our overdrafts. In the same way those from whom we buy the goods we need are themselves not going to find it so easy to borrow from the bank and will therefore be unable to give us the long credit that we have had in the past". Does anyone reading this think that the current (2011) complaints from businesses heard during the present financial crisis is a case of history repeating itself?

A COURAGEOUS MOVE IN DIFFICULT TIMES

For some considerable time the Lea Valley Growers had talked about ways of improving the efficiency of their marketing and distribution and, in the midst of post-war austerity, at a time when many businesses were waiting for things to perk up, they made a bold and courageous move to turn discussion into reality.

On Thursday 24th April 1952, at precisely twelve noon, Sir James Turner, President of the National Farmers' Union, accompanied by Lady Turner, declared the newly built Packing Station and offices of Nursery Trades (Lea Valley) Ltd., situated in Crossbrook Street, Cheshunt, open. After proposing a toast to the success of Nursery Trades Sir James went on to say, "Let me say I deem it a privilege to have been asked to open this very fine packing station. I say this, not because it is the accepted thing to say in the circumstances, but because I am happy to take part in this ceremony which marks the beginning of a very important chapter in the history of your co-operative".

The forming of a co-operative venture, for the Lea Valley Growers would have been a major, and probably a much-debated, undertaking before actually making the decision to set the idea in motion. Although the growers had come together as an Association in 1911 to generally improve their growing and trading conditions, the evidence suggests that they still wished to operate very much as separate businesses.

The co-operative idea was first put into practice in England in 1844 by the Rochdale Pioneers and was a consumer-based enterprise. Since then the movement has expanded through different models from the various Co-operative Retail Societies to the John Lewis Partnership. Within the European Union the co-operative model is very strong in countries like France, Spain and Italy particularly in wine-producing, horticultural and agricultural regions.

Examining the speech of Sir James also allows us to understand some of the other challenges facing Lea Valley growers at the time and it is therefore worthwhile reproducing a short section of it here:

"At the present time the nation is again up against a financial crisis. It will be recalled that in November last the Government announced that in order to improve our balance of payments position it had been decided to revoke the open general licences under which a whole host of commodities had previously been imported and to restrict imports by the issue of licences for specific quotas. The principal glasshouse crop affected for which imports will be restricted is cucumbers, the quota figure for which has been fixed at £60,000 for the period 2nd June, 1952, to 31st December, 1952, against a figure of £145,148 for the comparable period last year.

The Nursery Trades (Lea Valley) Limited new Packing Station, Crossbrook Street, Cheshunt, April 1952.

Tomatoes have been the subject of a previous announcement and the same arrangements as operated in 1951 will apply,

i.e.:

16th June to 30th June imports will be 3,600 tons

1st July to 31st July imports will be 7,200 tons

1st August to 31st August imports will be 2,300 tons

1st September to 15th October imports will be Nil

I would, however, emphasize that the reduction in imports following the Chancellor's November statement is purely fortuitous due to the country's difficulties. As a long-term measure designed to improve stability within the industry the Union feels that an adjustment of specific duties to give them the same effect as pre-war is the best method of regulating imports in the interests of the consumer and the grower. We all know the difficulties which attach to the system of quantitative regulation and it is our earnest hope that the Government will restore the effectiveness of import regulation based on specific duties."

In responding to Sir James's speech, the chairman of Nursery Trades, R E Fouracres, showed his appreciation for the work of earlier members when he said "Nursery Trades owes its birth to the Lea Valley Growers' Association, for it was in 1921 that a committee of that body set up our trading organisation to combat price rings which threatened commodities used by nurserymen". He then went on to say, "The names of the pioneers are still with us, and will always be, and the Rochfords, Hakanssons, Shoults, Larsens, Cobleys, etc., will be remembered for the manner in which they led us along the right lines upon which we have developed. At the same time, combine selling was being operated by Glasshouse Growers' Sales Ltd., and it was only natural that fusion would take place, and 1947 saw the amalgamation of two successful societies under our present name".

Within his response the chairman of Nursery Trades reported that the Lea Valley had the "largest concentration of glass in the United Kingdom" and he also went on to say that it produced "twenty-five to thirty thousand tons of tomatoes annually with a further twenty thousand tons of cucumbers and about a million pounds worth of flowers and pot plants, raised by more than five hundred growers", and this produce, he explained, "finds its way, often through two or three hands into nearly every

market in England and Wales". Having highlighted the present position of the Lea Valley horticultural industry, which on the face of it looked extremely encouraging, there is little doubt that Fouracres saw no room for complacency. This becomes clear when Fouracres made what can only be described as a stinging criticism of his industry when he said "there is little evidence of any planned policy in marketing or transportation. Neither is there standardization of grading or packaging. In each of those fields the foreigner leaves us cold". It must be remembered that this would have been a well-prepared response by the chairman and not something that had been thought up on the spur of the moment.

There seems little doubt that the Lea Valley Growers' Association had recognised the formidable challenges which lay ahead, particularly those coming from the Dutch growers who had efficiency of scale on their side and the added advantage of being able to ship produce to British markets within hours of gathering.

By building the new packing station the growers had begun to address the threats that were mounting from the overseas growers, but the question was whether this initiative had come too late to prevent future nursery closures. The Association had also taken the opportunity to vacate their premises at 126 Crossbrook Street, which was then leased to a local business, and move into a modern suite of offices within the new packing station building. This move would ensure improved and speedier communication and also make the administration of the Association more efficient.

THE CONTINUING PROTECTION DEBATE

The most regularly reported single topic in the Association's News Letters of the early 1950s are questions raised by members and the continuing debate about of how the British horticultural industry should be protected against foreign imports. Tariffs on imported produce tend to be favoured by the growers while the government tries to address the problem by introducing produce quotas. Although the government often makes promises to the growers that the import quotas will be reviewed and adjusted in the light of crop fluctuation, this system tends not to work as it is impossible to respond quickly to a sudden glut or down-turn in the home supply. Members of Parliament and Ministers are regularly lobbied with regard to these issues by the Association and also through the National Farmers Union.

Another clever ploy in the produce protection fight that was often employed was to invite the Minister of Agriculture or a high-ranking official to the Association's annual dinner and in the response to his after-dinner speech raise the question of tariffs. In fairness there was a problem for the government in dealing with this issue to the satisfaction of the growers. Trade agreements made after the Second World War, particularly with Europe and America, had really limited their options.

Television and radio programmes were used by the Lea Valley growers to get their story across regarding import tariffs.

When R E Fouracres, chairman of Nursery Trades, made his remarks about the British horticultural industry that "there is little evidence of any planned policy in marketing" he may have had a valid point. As far back as 1929 there had been in place the Merchandise Marks (Imported Goods) No. 4 Order, which required an "indication of origin" on produce. This meant that either the word "Empire" or "Foreign" would have to be displayed or the actual country of origin clearly marked and securely attached to the outside of any container of produce. Furthermore, should imported produce like tomatoes etc. be displayed in shops or on a street stall or barrow, a show ticket giving the indication of origin, in letters not less than half an inch high, had to be clearly visible. Failure to comply with the Order was an offence under the Merchandise Marks Acts which carried a penalty.

When Fouracres referred to "little evidence of any planned policy in marketing", perhaps he was thinking that all home-grown produce should clearly specify that it was English or British at point of sale. In other words the way to market home-grown produce was by giving the customer the opportunity to support the local nursery industry by having a choice between British, Empire or Foreign.

In the July 1953 News Letter an invitation was extended to members to join a specially chartered British Railways train that would take them from Euston (picking up en route at Bletchley, Rugby and Stafford) to the National Farmers' Union Annual Agricultural Show to be held at the Blackpool Show Ground. The cost of the ticket was four guineas, (four pounds and four shillings). This included return train fare from London to Blackpool, with a light breakfast and a full lunch on the train. Also included was the return bus journey from Blackpool Railway Station to the Show Ground with entrance fee. On the journey back to London dinner was to be served in the dining car. Although the amount of money involved for such a day out would seem an absolute bargain in comparison to today's prices, this would have represented a high proportion of the wage of an average working man.

Before the July Executive Committee of the Association took place a talk was given by C E Hudson, of the Ministry of Agriculture and Fisheries, the subject of which concerned the work being done "regarding the provision of Experimental Stations, Advisory Services, research Stations and Demonstration Centres" throughout the country. Lieutenant Colonel Leach, Chairman of the Executive Committee, stated that the "Lea Valley would be shortly losing Cheshunt and had nothing yet to replace it". He went on to say that "Cheshunt had long ceased to be an advisory centre and was devoted to research work".

It was made clear to Hudson that the growers required a facility where they "could go with their problems and receive on the spot advice". In recent times the growers were reliant on commercial undertakings to get the advice they required. Hudson responded by explaining that "under the auspices of the National Agricultural Advisory Service, the Ministry was in the process of acquiring land in the Lea Valley upon which it was intended to erect a laboratory for the housing of a pathologist and a chemist". This, he said, "would be the first step to provide an on the spot service, and it was hoped also to provide, at a later stage, an experimental station of glasshouses on the same piece of land". In an article by a "special contributor" in the September News Letter it was stated that it was common knowledge that the Cheshunt Research Station would shortly be moving to Sussex. The article went on to explain that the "Ministry of Agriculture hopes (when the financial situation permits) to establish a glasshouse experimental sub-station on a site a few miles north of Cheshunt". In fact, growers had to wait until 1958 before the Experimental Horticultural Station opened in Ware Road, Hoddesdon.

Since the Lea Valley Growers' Association first formulated plans to establish an Experimental Research Station at Cheshunt as far back as 1912 and then financed the project, it would appear from the above comments, and various inputs from the Ministry of Agriculture, in the intervening years, that this latter body had taken over the responsibility of running the Experimental Research Station and the other advisory services.

It will be recalled that in April 1952, after much pomp and ceremony, Nursery Trades (Lea Valley) Ltd. had moved into a brand new purpose built packing station in Crossbrook Street, Cheshunt. Three years later, and much to my surprise, we discover that Nursery Trades had vacated the Crossbrook Street premises and had bought the former Experimental Research Station building at Turners Hill, which was now standing vacant after the service had been moved to Sussex. The Lea Valley Growers' Association, now being without a home, were offered temporary accommodation on site in a building that once housed the National Agricultural Advisory Service. This they took up and on 1st October 1955 and once again began providing a service to their members.

As the Association had leased its former offices at 126 Crossbrook Street to a local firm of heating engineers the Executive Committee decided that the time had come to sell the building and make provision to build new premises. A piece of land was acquired at Turners Hill, on which stood two old cottages, numbered thirty-seven and thirty-nine and this would become the site of the Lea Valley Growers' new home. In December 1955, when Joseph Rochford, the President of the Lea Valley Growers' Association, gave his report at the Annual General Meeting, he took the opportunity to describe to the members the type of accommodation that had been planned. He explained that plans had been passed by the appropriate authorities and a tender to build had been accepted. The offices would consist of "a small two-storey building which will have four small offices downstairs and a Board Room and a small room upstairs", it was also reported that work was due to start.

While Joseph Rochford, in his report, covered several other subjects of interest that had occurred during the past year, the one thing I found puzzling was that there was no mention of why Nursery Trades (Lea Valley) Ltd. had vacated their brand new state-of-the-art Packing Station after only three years. One can only speculate that the venture had been unprofitable which would suggest that not enough growers were using the facility or was it a case that the number of growers in the region was insufficient to load the Packing Station during the peak growing season?

Before Joseph Rochford gave his official report he briefly alluded to the great honour paid to him at the November annual dinner, held at the Savoy Hotel, when he was presented, on behalf of the Lea Valley Growers' Association, with a silver salver by Sir James Turner, President of the National Farmers' Union. This was to commemorate Joseph's twenty-one years as President of the Association.

In Sir James's speech that followed he stated that he "believed that there was still a big future for the horticultural industry in this country". He also said that "we as a nation were facing a situation where we are living beyond our means, and the only way in which we can redress the situation is to earn more or spend less, live on tick or live on less. The horticultural industry had a tremendous job to do to spend less, in order to save foreign exchange by not having to spend on foreign products and to get the industry more competitive in order that entry could be made into world markets". Readers will no doubt recognise themes within Sir James's speech that echo the warning of politicians and economists today.

However, there was one small word within Sir James's speech that particularly attracted my attention as it seemed to indicate the speaker's reservations about the horticultural industry's future. That word was "still" and, when analysed in the context of, "there was *still* a big future for the horticultural industry", this might suggest that Sir James was issuing a veiled warning that economic storm clouds were gathering. The fact that he had introduced such a word suggests that the clock was ticking for the horticultural industry but there was only a little time left to turn things around.

We have now reached a three year hiatus in the Association's News Letters, but fortunately some of the gap can be filled in by referring to the *Special Edition of the News Letter* that was produced in 1961 to commemorate the golden jubilee of the Lea Valley Growers' Association. Here we learn that in 1956 a highly risky initiative was started by a number of Lea Valley flower growers who had banded together to explore the possibility of exporting blooms to Canada. The cost of the experiment was borne entirely by these growers who had set themselves up as British Flower Exports. After sending a number of consignments by air freight the idea was soon abandoned as it was reported that the growers had suffered "quite substantial losses". The initiative probably indicates that at the time profit margins were tight in the home markets and the flower growers were desperate to find alternative outlets.

During 1956 a party of about forty farmers from America visited nurseries in the Lea Valley and this was followed by another group from Holland. Not to be outdone, in July, a party of Members of Parliament, representing the Conservative Horticultural Committee, spent a day visiting nurseries in the Lea Valley and they also held talks with members of the Association's Executive Committee. To show that they were even handed, and indicating, in my view a high degree of political astuteness, the following month the Executive Committee invited "a similar party from the Socialist benches" and it was reported that "fifteen Labour Members came down to the Lea Valley".

In 1957 the Lea Valley Growers' Association moved into their newly built offices at 37/39 Turners Hill, Cheshunt, the same building that the Association occupies today. The total cost, which included the purchase of land, the demolition of the two cottages and the construction of the new building came to £8,380 18s 7d, a ridiculously low sum in comparison with what the project would have cost today. Also in this year we begin to see the veiled predictions, that had been made by Sir James Turner a little over a year before, come to fruition as the

An artist's impression of the new building at Turners Hill, Cheshunt, in the mid 1950s, much as it looks today.

Special Edition of the News Letter reported "the beginning of the large scale disappearance of nurseries which was a sure sign that the industry had become less prosperous, and many of the holdings were old and played out". Here we see the first cracks appearing in the Lea Valley glasshouse industry and the beginning of a decline that would continue into the future for some time.

For many years the nursery industry had lobbied government to impose strict tariffs on foreign imports of produce, and was still in the process of doing so, with little success, but in my view this was not the solution to the long-term viability of the industry. The clue is given in the *Special News Letter* when the anonymous writer remarks that "many of the [nursery] holdings were old and played out". In other words a number of growers, probably the smaller ones, had not invested and modernised their businesses and had not kept up with technological improvements. This trend was not just a phenomenon of the Lea Valley horticultural industry; it was a widespread problem throughout British industry in general, particularly in the first three decades after the Second World War.

Before the war British industry had a foothold in many markets around the world, but post-war this had changed as overseas customers discovered other ways of obtaining goods and services, many modernising their own industries or starting up new manufacturing facilities, often with the support of their banks who made the necessary finances available at low rates of interest. Once their new industries were established, these countries could often produce goods that were cheaper and more reliable than those made in Britain. This allowed them to compete, not only with Britain's traditional markets but with our home market as well. The trouble for Britain was that our captains of industry had not recognised or had ignored the problem and carried on regardless in the same old arrogant way as if the world owed Britain a living. Unfortunately this philosophy was carried forward into the home market through products that were unreliable, of poor quality and expensive to buy. Believe me, during my days in industry, I have witnessed these events first hand.

In May 1957 foreign tomatoes were dumped onto the British markets in great quantities and this must have dealt a severe blow to the confidence of the Lea Valley growers and in particular to those smaller growers who were already considering whether it was worthwhile staying in the horticultural industry. Representation was made to the local Member of Parliament for East Hertfordshire, then Secretary of the Board of Trade,

Sir Derek Walker-Smith, but nothing seems to have happened. The following year, more growers left the business, probably influenced by a particularly cold, wet summer which for them would have been the last straw.

As 1959 dawned, the Lea Valley Association's received further bad news when the Board of Trade announced that there would be "no alteration" to the import duties on foreign tomatoes. Interestingly, the final paragraph of the Board of Trade's rejection letter, which I reproduce here, tends to support my earlier suggestion that import tariffs would not provide a permanent solution to the Lea Valley horticultural industry's continuing problems.

"In reaching their decision, the Government have taken account of the special difficulties confronting certain sectors of the horticultural industry, but they consider that these difficulties are not of a kind for which tariff increases are the right remedy. The Minister of Agriculture will be making an announcement in the House on Monday on the Government's policy towards horticulture."

The growers' response to the government's rejection was one of fury. A special meeting of the National Farmers' Union Horticultural Policy Committee was called and also an emergency meeting of the Glasshouse Produce Committee and the following blistering statement was issued.

"The three UK Farmers' Unions do not accept the Government's reasons for rejecting their application for tariffs on cauliflower, broccoli, lettuce and endive. They are firmly convinced that there is an irrefutable case for revised tariffs – especially on tomatoes".

No doubt stung by the speed and ferocity of the growers' response the Minister of Agriculture, John Hare, announced that he would be making an "informal visit" to the Lea Valley on 30th January "when he will call upon growers for the purpose of meeting them and chatting on their nurseries".

In the meantime the government had announced the introduction of a seven and a half million pound Horticultural Improvement Grant Scheme, over the next five years, to help the rebuilding of glasshouses, upgrade heating systems and to improve grading and presentation of horticultural produce. On the face of it one would have expected the news to have been greeted with joy, but the Association's reaction to the scheme was to communicate to the Minister, in no uncertain terms, that this approach to their problems was not required and the only support that they wanted was for the government to impose tariffs on foreign horticultural imports. The tariff row rumbled on throughout the year with resolutions being passed at the NFU Annual General Meeting calling for the Union to press the government "for immediate action" on the question of tariffs. Even two of the growers got the opportunity "to express deep disappointment regarding the tariff rejection" on *Round and About*, a BBC Television programme. All this anger and frustration, in my view, was a distraction for both the NFU and the Lea Valley Growers Association as it diverted the focus of attention away from horticulture's more pressing and immediate problems.

However, the year did bring some glimmer of joy to hearts of the Lea Valley growers when Her Majesty Queen Elizabeth, The Queen Mother, made a tour of the region's nurseries in June. Apparently the Queen had personally requested the tour which concluded with a tea party, held on the sports ground of Messrs Joseph Rochford at Turnford.

A LORD'S WARNING

In his fifteenth annual speech to the National Farmers' Union in January, 1960, the President, Lord Netherthorpe – 6th January 1908 to 8th November 1980 – (formerly Sir James Turner), warned members of his extreme anxiety when he said:

"…we must continue to keep the most careful watch on agricultural development in Europe. I must confess that I am extremely anxious about a Europe divided between 'Six' and the 'Seven'. Agriculturally, we are at the receiving end. If for example, under their new common agricultural policy, which involves the use of the complete apparatus of price support and import control, the Six expand their production, there will be nothing to stop the surplus from arriving on our market".

The 'Six' which Lord Netherthorpe referred to were the European States of Belgium, France, Italy, Luxembourg, Netherlands and West Germany who, on 25th March, 1957 signed the Treaties of Rome, that came into effect on 1st January 1958 and established the European Common Market, which we now know as the European Union.

What had clearly concerned Lord Netherthorpe was

Lord Netherthorpe, then Sir James Turner, presenting Bernard Rochford with a silver salver to commemorate twenty-one years' service as President of the Lea Valley Growers' Association.

that Belgium and the Netherlands, two of Lea Valley Growers' biggest horticultural overseas threats, were among those early members of the European Union. Netherthorpe was convinced that the Six were apt to expand their production over the next few years and would most likely be looking for "export outlets outside the Community".

In concluding his speech, Netherthorpe had some sound advice for the long-term survival of Britain's agricultural and horticultural industries when he made four very knowledgeable and telling points.

First, he expressed the view that:

"In Europe we must work for a European agricultural agreement between the Six and the Seven. If we do not achieve this, we are likely to be the main sufferers from the diversion of agricultural trade emerging from the economic division of Europe".

Second he made the point that

"…our role on the domestic front is to produce from our limited acres as efficiently as we are able by applying technical improvements, and by the most economic use of resources to reduce our unit costs of production. To this end the availability of adequate capital, properly used as a tool of good management is vitally necessary".

The third piece of advice was

"…we must also adapt our production, as to quantity, type, quality and consistency, to meet the challenge of developing and changing consumer demands. The prospects of achieving this on a sufficiently broad scale are bedevilled by the fact that our industry is composed of a multiplicity of small and thereby weak, individual enterprises. Collective effort, the only source of greater strength, and its growth, is conditional upon real cohesion, involving as it does either some willing sacrifice of unfettered independence or agreement to statutory enforcement through agricultural marketing legislation".

And last but not least Netherthorpe made a rather telling observation when he said:

"Failure to co-operate means inevitably the clash of interests and the encroachment on each others' field of endeavour. Vertical integration in itself [is] no solution even though in other countries it may have proved a threatening menace. Forward thinking in joint endeavour offers more fruitful prospects".

It is interesting to note how visionary Netherthorpe was in his outlook and his analysis of his beloved industry. Here he had identified areas of concern such as the European Union, technical improvements, changing consumer demand and the need for co-operation that posed threats and challenges for the future British agricultural and horticultural industries.

In February 1960 the new Agricultural Wages Order came into operation which brought in a minimum rate of pay for a forty-six hour week. For a male over the age of twenty the rate was eight pounds and for a female over twenty-one six pounds, one shilling and six pence. Boys between fifteen and sixteen were to be paid three pounds thirteen shillings and six pence while girls of the same age were to receive three pounds, five shillings and six pence.

The March News Letter includes a short article entitled *Gunpowder Factory – Experimental Explosions*. Here we learn that members of the Association in the Waltham Abbey area are "perturbed about the vibrations caused by explosions at the Gunpowder Factory. Many instances of cracked glass and slipping squares have been experienced". Members who wished to make a claim were advised to forward this to the Association and it would then be passed to the Ministry of Supply. It is known that the Royal Gunpowder Mills used to carry out experimental under-water explosions at the north end of the Waltham Abbey site at a facility called Newton's Pool. Perhaps it was these explosions that were causing the local growers' problems?

For many years, along with the National Farmers' Union, the Lea Valley Growers' Association had been lobbying government to have an extra duty levied on foreign tomatoes arriving in Britain. On May 5th 1960, much to the relief of the Association, the government announced that two pence would be levied on each pound of imported tomatoes during "certain periods of the season". However, in the budget the following year, it was announced that there would be an extra two pence duty per gallon levied on fuel oil. Naturally the growers were up in arms over the increase as it was argued they had been encouraged by government to switch away from solid fuels to make economies and to change to oil as an alternative means of heating their glasshouses. The reader will no doubt recognise that when governments try and balance the books it is normally inevitable that there will be winners and losers or, in some cases, stagnation.

A map showing the current (2011) member states of the European Union.

When making his speech at the Association's thirty-seventh annual dinner in November 1962, held at the Savoy Hotel, Lieutenant Colonel Leach, Chairman of the Executive Committee, expressed his reservations about Britain's entry into the European Common Market when he said, "Now, the negotiations for British entry to the Common Market give rise to problems for British horticulture unparalleled in our history. As you well know, I have strong reservations on the matter both on broad constitutional and commonwealth grounds". In his reply, on behalf of the guests, Harold Woolley, President of the National Farmers' Union, referred to the Union's stand, "which is very firm, regarding the Common Market" and made the following revealing statement "If for reasons outside our responsibility, the government embarks on great changes, we shall see that we do not seek to exonerate themselves from the pledges that they have given. We shall do all we can to see the Common Market arrangements recognise horticulture's position, and that the government does not ride off on the excuse that circumstances have changed". These types of feelings were widely held at the time and the topic of the Common Market still evokes considerable emotion today, even in polite circles.

In an article entitled *Growers Must Face Greater Demand for Standardisation*, in the December 1962 News Letter, Eric Gardiner, Chairman of the National Farmers' Union Central Horticultural Committee, made some extremely far-sighted observations when he wrote:

"We have seen come into being chain stores and supermarkets, which have moved into the realm of fruit and vegetable selling, even in a few isolated instances into flower selling. It seems almost certain that this method of selling will develop appreciably and ultimately we may well see some forty to fifty percent of our fruits and vegetables sold in this way, though nothing like that for flowers".

He then went on to say "This must lead to a greater demand for the standardised product – a greater demand for the product that can be bought on sample". Growers will no doubt recognise how right Eric Gardiner was.

At the 1965 Annual General Meeting of the National Farmers' Union two interesting resolutions were moved by representatives of the Lea Valley Growers' Association. These resolutions open a window on the membership's concerns regarding the future of the horticultural industry. In the first it was proposed that: "This Annual General Meeting, whilst welcoming the move of Covent Garden Market to a new site south of the Thames,

urges the National Farmers' Union to investigate the possibilities of setting up a market in the North London area". Here we see that the Lea Valley growers are losing their traditional market and they now want a replacement facility that is nearer to their nurseries.

Construction of the New Covent Garden Market began on a fifty-seven acre site at Nine Elms, Battersea in 1971 and the market officially opened for trade in 1974. In 1991 the old Spitalfields Market was relocated to a thirty-one acre site at Leyton, in the London Borough of Waltham Forest. The market is now referred to as the New Spitalfields Market. Originally located just outside the City of London, the market can trace its origins back to 1638. It was Charles I who gave a licence for "flesh, fowl and roots" to be sold, on what was then, Spittle Fields. Interestingly the site in Leyton now borders the northern end of the 2012 Olympic Park.

The Old Spitalfields Market at the beginning of 20th century.

The New Spitalfields Market, Leyton as it appears today (2011)

The second resolution was quite different and is centred on the question of tariffs, but on this occasion, ironically ones that were imposed on British produce. "This Annual General Meeting deprecates the import regulations operated by other countries, including the Commonwealth, which makes it difficult for British growers to export their produce, and urges either greater facilities be afforded to the Home Industry or the British Government should impose similar restrictions on imports to the United Kingdom." This is a classic example of the consequences of placing tariffs on imports. Retaliation by the overseas countries is sure to follow and the restrictions imposed may not be directed just towards horticultural products.

When Bryan F Meering was elected Chairman of the Association's Executive Committee, at the Annual General Meeting in February 1965, he immediately, with the encouragement of the Executive's members, took the unusual step of publishing a four and a half page article entitled, "Why can't the Lea Valley…?" in the Association's March *News Letter*. In fact the Committee were so enthusiastic for Meering's article they arranged for reprints to be made as in their words "the wider the circulation of this information the better".

Bryan F Meering was elected Chairman of the Lea Valley Growers' Association in 1965.

So what was so important about the content of the article that made the Executive Committee want to distribute it to a wider audience? Probably this is the first time that someone, at grass roots level, had carried out an analysis of the horticultural industry over a period of ten years. Here Meering had shown how the tonnage of imported produce such as cucumbers, particularly from Holland and Spain, had increased astronomically from 21,009 hundredweight in 1954 to 379,741 hundredweight in 1964. He had also looked at a range of other statistics that had affected the competitiveness of British horticulture from the cost of labour to the price of anthracite and had woven his arguments together in a pretty comprehensive document.

In Meering's conclusion to his article he warns of impending disaster for the horticultural industry and returns to the old worn-out argument that called for import tariffs. While I believe this proposal is flawed I think that the article did bring about a watershed moment in the fortunes of the Lea Valley horticultural industry. At around the time of the article's publication the Lea Valley horticultural industry had begun to show the first signs of a slip that would gain momentum, becoming a serious slide in the membership of the Association. At its peak in 1962 the Lea Valley Growers' Association could boast a healthy membership of 550. A little over four decades later the membership figure was down dramatically to 110, a massive fall of eighty percent.

My first impression of Bryan Meering, as the News Letter had given nothing away regarding his background, was that he was probably someone from outside the horticultural industry. This had been based on the assumption that Meering clearly had the ability to take a step backwards to complete his analysis of the industry. While Lord Netherthorpe, in his farewell speech in 1960 had flagged up the deep-rooted problems within the industry, it was Meering who took a more critical look at the overall difficulties that were endemic and he identified the challenges facing the Lea Valley horticultural industry in the future. However, I later discovered my assumption that Meering was an outsider had been entirely wrong as he had been an industry insider all along.

I was fortunate in being able to speak to Ruth Halladey, a member of staff at the Lea Valley Growers' Headquarters at Turners Hill, who was employed by the Association at the time of Meering's Chairmanship. Not only did Ruth know the man but she told me her mother had been in service to the Meering family and had often babysat young Bryan. She further explained that Meering had a nursery in Cheshunt, E F Meering Ltd., specialising in roses and she believed that he may have owned another nursery at Waltham Abbey. Ruth also mentioned that Bryan's brother Ralph ran a local company supplying conveyor belt equipment to the horticultural industry that was used by growers for grading and packaging operations.

Stan Newens, MP for Epping standing beside Bryan Meering, Chairman of the Lea Valley Growers' Association, sitting to the left of picture. Mr Meering appears particularly pleased with what he is hearing

ANOTHER GREAT BLOW TO THE LEA VALLEY HORTUCULTURAL INDUSTRY

With Meering's analysis still ringing in growers ears and the mounting pressure on the Lea Valley horticultural industry from imports it might have seemed that within the next few years the once profitable nurseries would go the same way as other British industries in the post-war period of the 1960s and 1970s. Certainly the future of the Lea Valley horticultural industry looked exceedingly bleak as I learned from Thomas Rochford, the last Managing Director from the Turnford dynasty of Rochfords, who took over the chairmanship of the Lea Valley Growers' Association in 1980. Thomas recalled that when he took on his new role many members of the Association were in considerable financial difficulty.

A sea of glass, how the Lea Valley looked in its heyday.

Not long before, the Lea Valley nursery industry had been at the lowest point in its seventy year history after suffering one of nature's major disasters. In January 1976 the Lea Valley was hit by a massive storm with gale force winds, the like of which had not been experienced in the lifetime of the Association. Between three hundred and fifty to four hundred acres of glasshouses were completely flattened and their contents rendered useless; pulverised and covered in shards of glass splinters. The nurseries in the Broadly Common area of Essex were the worst affected where the scene of broken glass and levelled wooden structures was something akin to the London blitz. Tony Stevenson, who had only been in post as secretary of the Lea Valley Growers' Association for one month, vividly remembers the occasion and described to me how the storm had affected the members.

By 6th of January seventy-five insurance claims were being processed by the Association and it was thought this number would quickly double. Nursery owners who had only lost glass were submitting claims of up to £400 while for those who had lost everything the amount being claimed might be as high as £15,000 per acre. Many growers were already experiencing financial hardship, due in the main to increases in the cost of heating oil and also from cost hikes in other goods and services. These had occurred over the previous eighteen months and some growers had risked not being insured or had taken out inadequate insurance cover for such an

After the storm 1976, the last straw for some growers.

unforeseen and rare event. For many of them the losses sustained were so great they had to leave the industry. Those who owned nursery land were in a slightly better position than those who rented as they could sell to the property developers and local authorities who were keen to build houses, both private and social, as the post-war boom took hold. But such amounts of money were little compensation for the years of dedicated toil that provided fresh produce for the markets of Britain.

For the British shopper the devastation in the Lea Valley would inevitably mean that prices for salad, fruit and vegetables would increase. On Tuesday 6th July the *Evening Standard* reported that "The news from Covent Garden today was that salads would be more costly for Londoners following the gales, because large sections of growing crops in Britain and on the Continent have been destroyed". David Middleton, a Covent Garden trader, was reported as saying "This type of weather hits the trade badly. For many people the winds and the rain have been disastrous. Crops have been reduced to pulp and smashed into the ground".

THE GROWERS TURN BOLSHIE!

The Lea Valley growers are not known for their left-wing leanings or for manning the barricades or picket lines, but in 1981 they became really animated and took their protests onto the streets. Tony Stevenson, the secretary of the Lea Valley Growers' Association at the time relates the story of when he accompanied the Growers on the protest.

In 1981 it was discovered that the Dutch glasshouse growers were receiving subsidised rates for their gas supplies which gave them a considerable financial advantage over growers of other member states within the European Union. This action was in contravention of the competition rules of the Treaty of Rome.

The Lea Valley Growers' Association took four coach loads of members to Brussels and joined with other growers from different parts of the UK to make their protest felt. Apparently the Association were the best organised and most numerous group taking placards and balloons, red ones representing tomatoes and green ones representing cucumbers. The placards carried the following slogans:

"If it's Dutch, don't touch"

"Cheap Dutch gas kills British growers"

"Goedkoop Hollands gas is dodelijk!"
(Dutch for 'cheap Dutch gas is deadly')

"Le gas Hollandais rompt le marche"
(French for 'Dutch gas breaks/breaches [ruins] the market. This was apparently a play on words with "market" representing the horticultural market generally, but more to the point the Common Market).

Tony explained that the protest in Brussels was the culmination of considerable political activity, and was ultimately successful, as the subsidy was eventually removed.

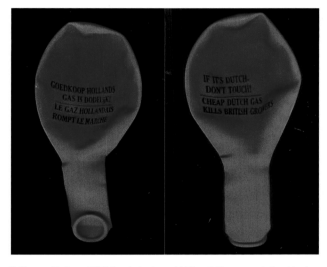

Balloons with slogan 'If it's Dutch don't touch'. These balloons were inflated in the back of a large covered lorry before the demonstration began.

The Brussels demonstration of 1981 by the Lea Valley growers with red balloons representing tomatoes and green cucumbers.

A GLIMPSE OF THE FUTURE AND THE SHAPE OF THINGS TO COME

The post-war skilled labour shortages that held back the development of the Lea Valley horticultural industry were partially alleviated when Sicilian and other Italian men began arriving in the region during the 1950s. Many had been attracted here because there was little or no work in their home country and Britain was seen as an opportunity where jobs within the horticultural industry were plentiful and available.

It is probably fair to conclude that many of the early immigrants suffered disappointment and hardship on arriving in Britain as they had to comply with the strict terms and conditions of the 1919 Aliens Restriction Act and also the 1920 Aliens Order. This meant that on arrival in the Lea Valley region they had to register with the police and they also had to provide proof of financial support. Further obstacles were put in their way as it was necessary to have the backing of a UK resident before a work permit could be granted. Once these hurdles had been cleared and a job secured the immigrants were required to stay with the same employer for a period of four years otherwise their work permit would be revoked and they were obliged to return to their home country.

Through long hours and sheer hard work many of these Italians were able to save enough money to send for their wives and children. Once here they were able to resume their homeland custom of working as a family unit. By the mid 1960s several families who had put sufficient savings aside were able to acquire their own nursery businesses, normally bought from those Lea Valley growers who, for one reason or another, were quitting the industry. Those immigrants who did not have sufficient funds to buy businesses often overcame the difficulty by forming co-operative ventures with their fellow countrymen and sometimes they would rent glasshouse space from growers who wished to retire.

The spirit of community among the Sicilian and Italian growers ideally suited the Lea Valley glasshouse industry and, at a crucial time in the industry's development, in my opinion, saved the industry from complete collapse by creating a strong and identifiable core structure.

It will be recalled that in January 1960, when Lord Netherthorpe made his farewell speech as President of the National Farmers' Union, he made specific reference to the challenges that faced the horticultural industry in Britain. He had highlighted the need to develop technical improvements in how food was grown and also the necessity for co-operation within the industry

to counter future threats and challenges to the progress of British agriculture and horticulture. Four years after Netherthorpe had expressed these concerns it was Bryan Meering who had written his analysis of the Lea Valley horticultural industry which had also flagged up similar issues.

We have now seen the second generation of Sicilians and Italians take over their fathers' nursery businesses and like many younger generations throughout the world they are more comfortable with the new technologies. These they have applied and, in many cases, they have changed their fathers' enterprises out of all recognition. A number of these new-age growers have invested heavily in a series of high-tech glasshouses where aluminium has replaced the traditional wood in the construction and they have also installed the latest state-of-the art combined heat and power systems (CHP) to replace the old labour intensive and inefficient boiler heating systems. Here glasshouses with floor-spaces that are measured in acres rather than metres are growing peppers, cucumbers and other produce. Gas has taken over as the preferred fuel from the old solid fuel and oil burning systems that were employed to heat the glasshouses and the carbon dioxide (CO_2) produced in the process is cleaned then fed into the growing areas and is naturally absorbed by the plants during the day providing a very efficient method of carbon capture. Surplus electricity generated by these CHP systems is sold to electricity supply companies and fed into the national grid.

Plants are now grown in individual containers and each is automatically fed a controlled amount of water and nutrients. The containers, which are filled with a rockwool fibre mixture, rather than earth or compost, are placed on what are termed "raised gutters". Effectively these are exceptionally long shelves, suspended above the ground on a system of wire braces connected to the framework of the glasshouse. Some nurseries use a system of grow-bags which are planted with specially grown seedlings cultivated by specialist producers. For example crops like cucumbers grown in this manner can produce three quality crops in a season.

Remembering the British growers' long drawn-out protests to the government over cheap Dutch imports of salad vegetables and the organised protests on the streets of Brussels in 1981 by the Lea Valley Growers' Association, it is perhaps somewhat ironic that one of the first growers to experiment with the growing of lettuce by the system of hydroponics was a Dutchman.

Hydroponics is a method of growing plants using mineral nutrients in water without soil. The "raised gutter" system, mentioned above, is a typical example of the process operating commercially. As early as the eighteenth century nurserymen began to understand

The hanging gutter system in one of Valley Grown Nurseries massive glasshouses.

how plants absorbed their essential nutrients for growth through water. Soil acts only as a sort of reservoir for the nutrients but is not essential to growth.

Growing by the system of hydroponics has many advantages for the nurseryman. As already mentioned no soil is used; water is effectively recycled as it is kept within the system reducing the amount used and therefore lowering cost. Having the control of the nutrient levels also reduces cost, improves crop yield and releases less pollution into the environment. Not having soil allows better control of pests and diseases that could lay dormant in the ground then spring a nasty surprise on the grower.

L A Dingemans came to Britain in the early 1960s on a chance visit and liked the country so much that he decided to stay. He first started experimenting with the science of hydroponics as a way of growing vegetables for his personal consumption and after a period of considerable trial and error he reached a stage of reasonable success which gave him the confidence to try the system as a commercial enterprise. Len Dingemans set up his first nursery in Enfield on a four and a half acre site and he later took over a second nursery in the area. His extraordinary pioneering work allows the claim to be made that he was the first grower in the Lea Valley to employ hydroponics in the growing of commercial salad crops.

In 1978 Len invested heavily in building a brand new nursery at Darnicle Hill, Cheshunt where he erected large aluminium-framed glasshouses. Here he employed the system of hydroponics that he had developed in Enfield and this new venture specialised in the growing of lettuce on a very large scale.

A lettuce grown by such methods will typically be ready for harvesting after only four weeks and Len told me that he would grow eleven and a half crops of lettuce in a year. At the nursery's peak it was producing seven million lettuces a year and the whole crop was taken by Sainsbury's supermarkets. According to Len, in the early 1980s the British supermarkets were expanding at such a rate that he found it impossible to keep up with their demand for produce. He however took the decision not to expand the size of his business further to cope with the increasing demands from the supermarkets for fear of overstretching himself financially.

In the year 2000 Len took a well-earned retirement and sold the Darnicle Hill nursery to Mark Sheppard, his business manager, who has carried on the business under the name of L A Dingemans & Company Limited. I asked Mark if the nursery still specialised in producing lettuce on its former massive scale but he told me this had ceased due to strong foreign competition that made growing the crop unprofitable. However, he explained that he had been experimenting with a range of different leaf products and was currently having great success with what he termed "living lettuce" which he now supplies to the supermarkets complete with roots. This is yet another story of how many of the growers in the Lea Valley region have adapted to a volatile and constantly changing market, driven in the main by the consumer who is seeking a different and fresher eating experience.

Incidentally, when interviewing Len Dingemans I asked if he had attended the 1981 demonstration in Brussels to protest against his former countrymen in the Dutch nursery industry and their use of subsidised gas. "Of course", he said; "I was an officer of the Association at the time and they were competing against the British growers unfairly". He further commented that he was surprised at the power that the Lea Valley Growers' Association were able to wield as the gas subsidy was eventually removed. Len appeared very proud to be a Bolshie adopted Brit!

Modern glasshouses that operate the CHP system employ thermal screens. These have around an eighty percent light transmission and are fitted approximately 3.5 metres above ground level and 1.5 metres below the roof to reduce heat loss. The screens are computer controlled, as are most of the growing operations, which are pre-programmed by the grower to respond to the internal variations of temperature and light within the particular glasshouse. Naturally all these improvements have come at a cost and growers have had to raise millions of pounds to cover their investment but it is the only way for the horticultural industry in Britain to survive.

Science now plays a big part in maintaining a healthy glasshouse crop and chemical usage for pest control is kept to an absolute minimum. The modern grower uses a system of Integrated Crop Management (ICM) where biological predators are used to control the pests. This not only saves money by reducing the need for expensive chemicals it also provides a healthier product for the health-conscious consumer. Bees, nature's highly efficient pollinating insects, have been introduced into many of the glasshouses to ensure that the plants are fertilised as nature had always intended.

When entering one of these glasshouses for the first time I was almost overwhelmed, both by the vastness of the place and the industrial scale of plant growing. The clean and clinical conditions of the growing area were not unlike those one might find in a modern hospital. Another feature which I could not fail to notice was the distinct lack of labour. Of course labour has to be used to hand string the new cucumber plants and to take off excess leaves on others. When the growing seasons ends the plants have to be removed and composted and the glasshouses cleaned and sterilised to make the area ready for the next crop, but otherwise very little labour is required.

Bees, natures pollinating insects at work at Glinwell Nurseries. This is an example how a modern grower is helping the environment.

Darnicle Hill Nursery, Cheshunt where hydroponics were first used in the Lea Valley on a commercial scale.

THE RESEARCH JOURNEY

Writing the last chapter and reaching this later stage of the manuscript has caused me to ponder and reflect on the changes in business attitudes and strategies that I discovered as I travelled through a century of dusty minute books, reports and newsletters. When I began the research I had no idea where the path would lead or what I would find as I followed the progress of the growers on a journey of discovery. In fact it was only when I visited the business of Valley Grown Nurseries, run by the energetic and knowledgeable Gary Taylor, when the "eureka" moment occurred, leading me to the realisation that my research had identified the very building blocks which were necessary for a healthy and sustainable horticultural industry. Valley Grown Nurseries was a prime example of what can be achieved by putting into practice lessons and systems that have been learned by the Lea Valley Growers' Association only in the last few decades.

It has been rewarding to discover a grower, and he is by no means the only one in the Lea Valley, who has implemented just about all the positive things I encountered through research which were required for creating a sustainable nursery business. These were, investing in and embracing new technologies like CPH and ICM systems, cooperating with other like-minded growers in the UK and overseas, sharing pack house and distribution costs, committing time to research and development programmes, putting in place improved industrial relations schemes and installing modern toilet and canteen facilities. In 2004 Valley Grown Nurseries received the coveted award "UK Salad Grower of the Year".

Valley Grown Nurseries represents a microcosm of best practice and demonstrates how other growers in the Lea Valley region are successfully adapting their businesses to meet the challenges of the modern world, driven by consumers who are demanding fresh and chemical-free produce, reduced transport miles and above all value for money.

Peppers being grown at Valley Grown Nurseries in computer-controlled glasshouses.

Gary Taylor Chairman of the Lea Valley Growers' Association and MD of Valley Grown Nurseries.

Valley Grown Nurseries, Nazeing.

Valley Grown Salads refrigerated transport.

A BIG IDEA

When speaking (August 2011) to Thomas Rochford, past chairman (1980 to 1987) of the Lea Valley Growers' Association, he explained that when he took over the chairmanship the financial plight of many of the members had caused him considerable concern. Not long before, the fifty-acre Turnford site that had been in his family for over one hundred years had been sold. By the 1970s the Turnford nursery was part owned by outside investors and it was these who were tempted to sell to the planners and developers who were hungry for building land. Many local people were saddened to see the once landmark area of glass cleared as house building began. Even the Rochford's ancestral home, Turnford Hall, fell to the developer's hammer. Fortunately the terraces of Turnford Cottages remain as a memorial to the Rochford family who built them for their workers.

With his beloved nurseries gone, Thomas was determined that the remaining Lea Valley nursery industry should not suffer the same fate. He also knew that if the Lea Valley horticultural industry overall was to decline further this could mean the end for the Lea Valley Growers' Association.

However, Thomas told me that he had been determined to turn things around and he had formulated an idea that might just work. He confessed that the scheme that he had in mind carried a certain degree of risk; and was not without its critics, even those close to him from within

his own family circle. Thomas had nurtured the notion that it was the post-war Italian growers that were the key to the Lea Valley's future horticultural success, but how could he light the fuse that would turn his thoughts into reality?

Any person studying the history of the Lea Valley Growers' Association up to the 1980s will soon discover that it was very much a gentleman's club. Photographs of social events like the Association's annual dinners at the Savoy and elsewhere always show a one hundred percent male audience. And it was probably these images that gave Thomas the idea to introduce events such as dinner dances that would make it more likely for women to attend.

Thomas wanted to particularly encourage the Italian growers to become more involved with the Association and making it easy for the whole family to attend social events was a simple way of achieving his goal. The dinner dances became extremely popular and many were over-subscribed. I suspect the formula worked well because it was natural for the early Italian families who came to the Lea Valley in the 1950s and 1960s to function as an integrated unit with a common work ethic. I believe that the philosophy of working together as a family unit also shaped a support structure for their fellow countrymen and created the platform for the Italian growers to develop and prosper. This is why this community represents by

Happy families, young Thomas IIII in the foreground with mum and dad at the family home.

Thomas III and Thomas IIII discuss house plants. Note the generational clothes gap!

far the most successful part of the Lea Valley horticultural industry today.

I was told by Thomas that his initiative to introduce women into the social life of the Association was not welcomed at the time by the traditionalists in the organisation and also some within his family. However, he is to be congratulated for bringing people kicking and screaming into a modern society where everyone is treated as equals. Although Thomas regrets the loss of his family business it did allow him to completely change his career path and he has now become a successful information technology consultant, travelling the country to design and also to troubleshoot existing hardware and software systems.

The Lea Valley Growers' Association annual dinner (1929) with not a woman in sight!

Thomas Rochford IIII in his home standing in front of his much loved aspidistra. It was Thomas who was responsible for setting a programme of dinner dances that first allowed wives to attend the once all-male preserve of the Association.

WHAT THE ROMANS DID FOR US

Romans who came to these shores almost two thousand years ago brought with them not only the technology to build roads, mills and canals but also introduced us to a range of foodstuffs that we enjoy today. These include, amongst other things, broad beans, carrots, celery, radish, cabbages and, perhaps most surprising of all, cucumbers! The Romans clearly recognised the strategic and agricultural importance of the Lea Valley region as they established ports and towns here and also built a road infrastructure to serve them.

In the late twentieth century it was other Italians who came to the rescue of the Lea Valley horticultural industry with their know-how and thirst for employing technology. They have created a breathing space for the nursery business in the region, allowing it to re-group and stabilise.

Sicilian and other Italian descendants now make up around ninety percent of the Lea Valley Growers' Association's membership and their presence has injected new energy into the local horticultural industry allowing it the opportunity to prosper. The remaining ten percent of the Lea Valley growers are also investing heavily in new technology and modern procurement systems while experimenting with new crops, such as herbs and aubergines, which are becoming more popular with the British consumer as the market looks for new tastes and eating experiences. This has been encouraged by the rash of cooking programmes now appearing on television and also the plethora of books, magazines and articles about the subject. Also, as many consumers now take their holidays abroad, their taste buds have been introduced to new eating experiences as fruits and vegetables not seen before in the UK make up some of the dishes served in hotels and restaurants.

A second-century AD Roman mosaic discovered at Verulamium (St Albans) by Sir Mortimer Wheeler in the 1930s.

A wall painting discovered in the ancient ruined city of Pompeii, Italy showing fruit. This was an important part of the Roman diet

A re-enactment of the Roman army in Britain by the Ermine Street Guard. This might have been the type of scene that locals would have witnessed almost 2,000 years ago.

A BRAVE NEW WORLD – A SMALL GROWER TAKES A BIG TECHNOLOGICAL RISK

In the early years of the twenty-first century, Guy & Wright Limited, a third generation family tomato growing business in Hertfordshire, owned by John and Caroline Jones, formed a partnership with Hennock Industries Ltd and New EnCo to develop a micro-turbine plant that would be powered from organic waste. To test the viability of the system a working commercial plant was installed, part funded by the Department of Trade and Industry (DTI) under the Technology Programme. After successful trials the plant was scaled up in size and John and Caroline took the bold decision to move away from fossil fuels as the main power source and to use them as an alternative only when the economics dictated.

To expand the system, known as anaerobic digestion (oxygen-free digestion) an enormous below-ground six-cell airtight bunker was constructed with each cell capable of holding four hundred tonnes of organic waste. In the process of organic matter decomposition a biogas is produced with high methane content and it is this gas which is compressed to directly drive the micro-turbines. This system of electricity production is more efficient and cleaner than the traditional methods of making electricity from natural or town gas. In this earlier technology gas is burned to heat water to produce steam which in turn drives turbines that are coupled to the electricity generators. With the new system the gas burning stage of the process is completely eliminated.

The anaerobic digester in use by Guy & Wright is an exceedingly greedy animal, requiring fifty tonnes of organic material per day to satisfy its hunger pangs. It will be appreciated that it would be impossible for the nursery to generate such a large daily amount of organic waste from its own operation, so arrangements have been made with London's Spitalfields Market, Bedfordshire Growers, who pre-pack onions, and banana importers J P Fresh of Dartford. These companies, and others, are all extremely

Gas turbines powered by methane vegetable waste that produce electricity to run the Guy & Wright nursery.

The plant room with equipment necessary for running the anaerobic digestion process.

An internal view of one of the six settlement tanks at the Guy & Wright nursery.

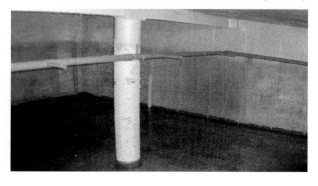

grateful to be able to donate their organic waste to Guy & Wright rather than send it to landfill which would incur them paying a levy. As an environmental initiative it is an all-round win–win situation.

Waste material coming to the nurseries is emptied by the delivery vehicles into a receiving pit and from there it slowly moves to a macerator where it is crushed and broken down into smaller pieces. The resultant "vegetable soup" is pumped into a holding tank before being distributed to the six underground digesting cells. This process is closely controlled by computer probes and only after testing and analysis does the required amount of material get fed to each of the cells. Waste residue from the cells is fed to three established reed beds, allowing the system to continuously supply gas without the need to shut down for cleaning. The biogas generated by the plant is fed into a giant inflatable bag which can then supply the five micro-turbines that produce the electricity and also a small boiler which is used to power the three miles of underground heating below the digestion cells. The CO_2 produced by the process is so clean, being mainly devoid of sulphur, it can be fed directly into the glasshouse growing area to be absorbed by the plants during the day without any form of treatment. This arrangement has considerably improved crop yield.

The installation of the plant, which began in 2003, took three years to complete with much of the construction work done by the Jones's and local specialist contractors. As expected, with a plant so unique, initial teething problems occurred and these had to be resolved alongside the Jones family running their business. In what appears to be an understatement, Caroline Jones says, "it [the plant installation] has been by no means easy" but now she concedes, with I suspect some relief, "we have achieved our goal".

Dr Andy Marchant of Hennock International Limited, the designer of the anaerobic digestion system at the nursery has claimed that "John and Caroline Jones were the first growers in the world to install micro-turbines with high rate CO_2 enrichment on a commercial nursery, and have been host to countless other growers keen to see what they were doing".

When the plant became fully operational the system produced more than enough electricity to satisfy the running of the nursery and the excess power was sold to Green Energy, a company that was established specifically to obtain and distribute electricity from renewable sources. This arrangement allows the Jones's to forget about the need for customer administration, with its inherent problems of metering and billing and to get on with the daily task of running their business.

For all their hard work, considerable financial expenditure and futuristic risk-taking John and Caroline Jones rightly deserved the prestigious Grower of the Year Awards 2009 – Business Initiative of the Year commendation.

There has been a decline in the number of Lea Valley horticultural growers over the past decade and the Jones's are the last remaining family owned tomato growers in Hertfordshire; but overall the other specialists are still supplying the UK markets with up to eighty percent of their cucumber requirements. Also it should be remembered that in the 1970s the yield for tomatoes grown in the region was approximately 70 tons per acre. Now, with the new technology, it is typically 280 tons, with more varieties grown to satisfy changing consumer demands.

It is not possible to predict the state of the Lea Valley horticultural industry over the next ten years, particularly in the current unprecedented harsh economic climate, but those remaining core of growers who have made the commitment to provide us with salads produced in the most environmentally friendly way deserve the support of all the retailers and also us, the consumer.

The reception area for vegetable waste at the Guy & Wright nursery.

Vegetable waste being dumped into tanks for bio gas production 2008.

A CHANGE IN CONSUMER REQUIREMENTS AND THE GROWERS' DILEMMA

Currently, environmentally aware consumers are making demands on retailers for more fresh produce that has been grown in Britain. Apart from home-grown food preserving the freshness and taste of the product it considerably reduces the high mileage the product has to travel. This helps to reduce the carbon footprint of food growing. I am constantly being told by growers that UK shops and supermarkets will take all the home-grown produce they can produce but in many cases the growers' hands are tied. The reasons for this are two-fold. Firstly technology has just about reached the maximum crop a grower can achieve in a specific area and there is therefore an urgent need to extend the growing area. This means building new glasshouses and this is where problem number two occurs.

Ironically, growers who want to increase the size of their nurseries to cope with consumer demand for British grown produce often fall foul of government and local authority planners who seem reluctant to sanction new build quickly. To help overcome these problems growers have resorted to snapping up just about every old nursery that comes onto the market in their quest to expand. Unfortunately these opportunities are few and far

Consumers are becoming aware that food travelling long distances is a serious threat to the world's carbon footprint.

between so growers frustratingly have to sit and twiddle their thumbs, or take the expensive option of moving their business to another part of the country. While these moves and delays are taking place the overseas growers can easily fill the supply gap.

An alarming story that I heard recently, which illustrates the planning morass that regularly heightens frustration levels amongst growers, was when a local authority gave planning permission to build a fifty-bed care home on land designated in the local plan for horticultural use.

People across the world are now looking for home-grown produce in their shops and supermarkets.

The site in question had once been occupied by a nursery which a number of local growers had wanted to buy to expand their businesses.

Not too long ago we could only buy fresh fruit and vegetables that were in season but all that has changed dramatically. When we walk into our local shop or supermarket we expect to be able to purchase all the different fruits and vegetables all the year round. Should we want to have fresh runner beans and garden peas and perhaps an exotic fruit with our Christmas dinner, then all we have to do is pop to the shop.

While our new-found habits as consumers have forced UK suppliers to look overseas for produce, our quest for the exotic has created an opportunity. British growers, particularly those new-age Sicilians and Italians in the Lea Valley have come up with a clever plan. While building their new pack houses for the purpose of quality assurance, packing, labelling and the distribution of produce, they have also invested heavily in horticultural production abroad and therefore have control of the out-of-season produce coming onto the British market. Sometimes these arrangements have been achieved through a joint venture with an overseas grower and on other occasions the growing facilities are wholly owned by the UK grower. Sometimes a co-operative venture is seen as the best way forward.

The costs of transporting produce to Britain can be high and the distance the produce has to travel will adversely add to atmospheric carbon, but it is not all bad news. Growing crops under glass in hot countries reduces the need to artificially heat the glasshouses and this in turn helps the industry to offset the damage to the environment as the necessity to burn fossil fuels is considerably reduced.

Throughout the history of the Lea Valley Growers' Association we have seen the constant battle to get the government to place import tariffs on foreign horticultural produce as a measure to limit the tonnage entering Britain. For example when Portugal and Spain joined the European Union in 1986 there was considerable anxiety amongst the growers that this would allow vast volumes of tomatoes and cucumbers to flood the British market. So concerned were the growers that these new members of the EU would seriously damage their livelihoods that a delegation from the Association gave evidence before a House of Commons Agricultural Committee to ensure the government quickly got the message. Later as the European Union's internal legislation progressed with the implementation of what was known as the "four freedoms" which seek to guarantee free movement of goods, capital, services and people, fresh concerns were felt in the Lea Valley.

However, when I was researching the recent developments in the horticultural supply chain for this book I quickly discovered that the new pack houses were sourcing produce from countries such as Holland, Spain, Poland, Morocco and Israel. While, at first sight, this might seem to be a case of, "if you can't beat them join them" in fact the philosophy behind these initiatives is a lot more sophisticated than it first appears.

The expansion of the European Union to its current (2011) twenty-seven members has not all been bad news for the Lea Valley growers. With an industry always desperate for a constant supply of reliable labour, particularly seasonal, it can be shown the European Union has come to the assistance of the Lea Valley growers. In 2004 Poland joined the European Union along with nine other European countries; Romania and Bulgaria joining in 2007. And it has been mainly Polish workers, over the last few years who have come to the rescue of both the horticultural and agricultural industry in Britain, filling an urgent labour shortage which for some reason had not been taken up by the indigenous workforce.

In my opinion, without the creation of these new initiatives with growers abroad the Lea Valley horticultural industry would be staring extinction in the face. As it is, this imaginative policy to source out-of-season and other crops from outlets overseas is working well and looks to be the way forward for the British horticultural industry. Hopefully the politicians will support the industry by implementing measures to resolve, ease and quicken the planning process to allow the Lea Valley growers to compete through economy of scale while their horticultural businesses still remain viable. With the demands of UK consumers, who are becoming more environmentally aware, the pressure is now on British growers to provide more and more home-grown produce. There is also an urgent need to feed a rapidly growing world population. Government must therefore give the British horticultural industry the opportunity to expand, compete and prosper.

As a National Farmers' Union survey discovered in 2008, government legislation was holding up the progress of the British horticultural and agricultural industries and costing growers considerable sums of money. Two-thirds of the members who responded to a questionnaire reported that they had lost income "as a direct result of labour shortage", each to the tune of £140,000 to September. Labour shortages could be filled by overseas workers but there are quotas placed on seasonal workers entering the country. An independent report, commissioned by the Migration Advisory Committee, a government advisory body, concluded that "the industry needs an improved version of the Seasonal Agricultural Workers Scheme (SAWS) to meet its labour demand – otherwise some growers are likely to quit labour-intensive crops while others will move more production overseas".

A RIGHT ROYAL OCCASION

On Tuesday 22nd February 2011, to commemorate the centenary of the Lea Valley Growers' Association, the Smallford Nurseries in St Albans were honoured by a visit from His Royal Highness, The Duke of Kent.

The Duke of Kent being introduced to members of the Lea Valley Growers' Association by their Chairman, Gary Taylor.

The Duke of Kent takes a keen interest in how tomatoes are grown.

Owned by Glinwell plc the Smallford Nursery occupies a site of some fifty acres growing cucumbers, peppers and tomatoes under glass. The site also includes storage and packing houses where produce is quality assured, graded and packed by employees using the latest processing machinery. The Duke was accompanied on a tour of the St Albans site by Glinwell directors Joe Colletti and Sam Cannatella and also by Gary Taylor, Chairman of the Lea Valley Growers' Association.

At the end of his tour the Duke was presented, appropriately with an engraved crystal salad bowl and a selection of salad produce as a memento of his visit. It was clear that the Duke had taken a great deal of interest in the nursery tour as he was seen to stop on several occasions to ask staff questions.

Afterwards an informal buffet was served and the Duke was shown a selection of photographs of Her Majesty Queen Elizabeth the Queen Mother, who had come to the Lea Valley in 1959. It is known that Her Majesty, apart from her love of horseracing, also had a keen interest in plants which would probably account for her personal request to tour the Lea Valley nurseries. The visit concluded with a tea party on the sports ground of the Rochford nurseries at Turnford.

The Duke's visit to Glinwell allowed me to see first-hand how this particular grower functioned and also gave me the opportunity to discuss the marketing strategy with senior members of nursery staff. Glinwell is one of those second generation Sicilian and other Italian family

The produce dispatch area at Glinwell Smallford Nurseries.

owned companies that has applied state-of-the-art technology and new ways of procurement and marketing (as discussed earlier) to the British horticultural industry and, in so doing, has become a successful and highly competitive organisation, which is one of the largest in the UK.

Since the late 1990s part of the Glinwell strategy has been to acquire nurseries within the UK (at the time of writing they have five) and to develop these businesses by dismantling the old wooden framed glasshouses and replacing them with modern structures and also installing new heating plant and other essential equipment. Large amounts of money have been ploughed into the expansion and development of these sites. In tandem with these UK acquisitions Glinwell have invested heavily in nursery businesses abroad and become involved in partnerships and joint ventures. Once these arrangements have been completed steps are then taken to expand and modernise the new businesses.

A key factor that had allowed Glinwell to invest so heavily is that in 1995 they took the decision to become sole supplier of Tesco, the UK's leading supermarket chain, founded by the entrepreneur the late Sir Jacob (Jack) Cohen. At first I considered this policy of putting all one's eggs in one basket a decidedly risky strategy to employ. However, it was explained that over the many years of supplying Tesco, before the sole supplier decision was taken, a strong bond of mutual trust and co-operation had been forged and now it would appear that this retailer has formed a very strong working relationship with Glinwell for their supplies of organic and conventional produce. When speaking to Glinwell staff one soon becomes aware that when consideration

is being given to plans for further expansion, Tesco is always at the forefront of their minds. Evidence for the relationship working well can be judged by the fact that Glinwell achieved the prodigious award, in 2008, of "Best Organic Supplier to Tesco" and in 2009 they received a "Lifetime Achievement Award".

The Duke of Kent is presented with a cut-glass salad bowl by Gary Taylor, Chairman of the Lea Valley Growers' Association.

Modern grading and packing facilities at Glinwell Smallford Nurseries.

The Duke of Kent signing the visitors' book to mark the centenary of the Lea Valley Growers' Association. Directors of Glinwell PLC, Joe Colletti and Sam Cannatella look on.

The Queen Mother admires the plants on her 1959 Lea Valley visit.

The Queen Mother
talks to members of
Thomas Rochford's
workforce. during
her 1959 visit

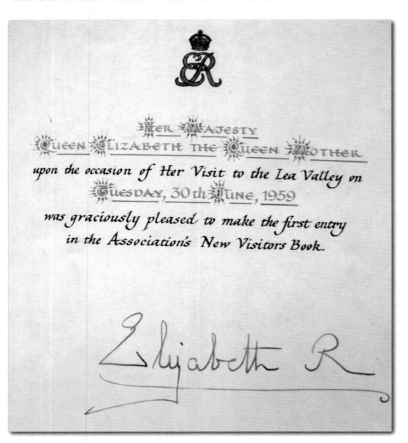

The Queen Mother records her visit to the Thomas Rochford nursery, Turnford, 30th June 1959.

Thomas Rochford III welcomes the Queen Mother to his Turnford nursery, 30th June 1959.

Tomato plants grown on a massive scale in one of Glinwell Nurseries. The entire operation is carried out in computer-controlled glasshouses.

A massive area of glass in North Africa, part of Glinwell Nurseries' overseas operation.

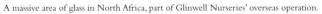

A DIFFERENT EXPERIENCE

For a number of years the Lea Valley Growers' Association, which the reader will recall is a specialist glasshouse branch of the National Farmers' Union, has been doing battle on behalf of the UK agricultural industry with the country's leading supermarkets over what they claim to be unfair prices paid for produce and also for the employment of bullying tactics. The issue recently came to a head with the publication of an article (3/7/2011) in a respected UK newspaper. The journalist interviewed a number of different farmers and producers covering the poultry, pig and dairy produce industries who all alleged similar claims of unfair treatment.

NFU Mutual

The emblem of the National Farmers' Union.

A poultry farmer from Devon claimed that problems began four years ago when the big egg packers merged and took control of around sixty percent of the market. This, it is suggested, took away competition and prices paid for products began to fall. At the same time other costs, including poultry feed prices, were increasing. The farmer complained that he was now only paid ninety-one pence a dozen for his large free range eggs when he had previously received over one pound for them. He remarked, "Meanwhile, my eggs were being sold for £3 [per dozen], while I was losing 15p on each dozen".

A North Yorkshire pig farmer who had been in business for thirty years complained on behalf of the industry,

"We had no help from the processors or the retailers at all and we've all been losing between £10 and £30 per finished pig". He went on to say "Usually in pork, the processor deals with the supermarket and he should represent us. But you'll never get a processor disagreeing with a retailer. The supermarkets play them off against each other on price – and the retailers bear down on any attempt to get the price up. But that's forcing producers out of business".

It was a similar story for a Cheshire dairy farmer who said

"Only of a quarter of the people round here who were in dairy 15 years ago are still doing it. In 1977, we got 25p a litre at the farm gate. We're getting 26p now. But the price in the shops then was 42p a litre and now it's anything from 70p to £1. And we've seen all the costs go up. Now we're selling to a milk broker. My milk might end up with supermarkets or Wiseman's. I'd rather be with Tesco or Sainsbury's, because they're guaranteeing 28p a litre to farmers. But they've capped the market because they're under pressure from Aldi and Lidl. The milk price could be much higher. You sign up to take whatever price the middlemen set and that can be retrospective. They might say, oh we're going to give you a penny less for June's milk, and there's nothing you can do about it. There's no negotiation. We couldn't survive without our pedigree bull business. The money for farmers has gone".

The article also pointed to a number of farmers who had spoken out about their alleged shabby treatment by the supermarkets but did not wish to be identified for fear of reprisal. One such story about an East Anglia poultry farmer who complained about bullying tactics and the system of negotiating outside contracts while he was attending an industry conference, reported that he had his next shipment of chickens to a retailer refused on spurious quality grounds.

While I am unable to verify any of the above stories I am certainly familiar with the demands placed upon suppliers and manufacturers by large retail outlets and their agents. When I worked in the consumer electronics industry we would often be approached by large retailers who would try and dictate the price that they wished to pay for a piece of radio or television equipment that they wanted to sell in their stores at a discount, below the recommended retail price. Often the prices offered would not cover the manufacturing and distribution overheads. Of course sometimes for some reason or another (normally if stock was piling up in the warehouse) the manufacture did sell at the retailers' take it or leave it price. If the deal went ahead there was the strong possibility that this would upset the many small independent retailers who had traditionally supported the manufacturer in times of hardship. These small independent dealers lacked the buying power of the big retail chains to obtain bulk discounts.

The newspaper article refers only to the difficulties experienced by the agricultural industry and does not have anything to say about the horticultural industry.

THE CENTENARY CELEBRATORY YEAR HAS BEEN MARRED!

Just as the Lea Valley Growers' Association was building up to celebrate its centenary year, something unexpected happened to dampen the party atmosphere.

In early May 2011 the German health authorities reported a severe outbreak of an illness called haemolytic-uremic syndrome (HUS), a type of food poisoning which affects the blood and kidneys and in severe cases the central nervous system. Later, on the 21st of the month, the first death from the condition was recorded. By May 26th the German authorities had announced that they had identified Spanish cucumbers as the source of the *E. coli* outbreak and promptly withdrew them from the market. Steps were also taken by the German authorities to alert nearby countries to the source of the outbreak.

As one might imagine, once the authorities had made their announcement the news spread like wildfire throughout the media with many exaggerated and unsubstantiated reports occurring across the world. The *Mail Online* ran a story on May 28th which claimed "A food poisoning bug found in organic cucumbers has killed five of its victims. Hundreds more have fallen ill in the outbreak, which could affect tomatoes and lettuce too". Television news pictures flashed across our screens showing Spanish horticultural workers dumping hundreds of tons of freshly picked and as we now know perfectly good cucumbers into skips. At the time I could not help thinking that the whole exercise was one of panic and not a rational overall scientific approach to discovering the true cause of the problem.

The European Commission announced that two glasshouses in the Andalusia region of Spain had been identified as the source of the outbreak and were closed while soil and water samples were analysed. These turned out to be clear of *E. coli* contamination and the focus was then turned towards cross-contamination of the produce in transit either on the way or within Germany.

Other suspected sources of the *E. coli* contamination were a nursery in Lower Saxony growing bean sprouts and also batches of fenugreek seeds imported from Egypt in 2009 and 2010 from which the sprouts were grown. The situation for the salad growers became considerably worse when the Robert Koch Institute in Germany advised against the consumption of raw cucumbers, lettuce and tomatoes. Clearly the authorities had mishandled the situation which was now out of control with the Spanish growers seeking compensation from the German authorities for their massive losses.

Unfortunately the losses had not only been felt in Spain but had also spread much further afield to the Lea Valley and beyond. The British health-conscious public were badly shaken by the E. coli scare that had been erroneously created by the German authorities. This coupled with the reports and the graphic images shown in the media of alleged contaminated produce being dumped had caused them to stop buying their usual quantities of salad produce. The effects of their actions quickly spread to Lea Valley growers who have seen their overall income reduced by an estimated one and a half million pounds a week. This has forced them to seek compensation from the European Union. Initially the European Union had proposed issuing a £135 million compensation package to help mitigate the losses of the growers but already some member states have claimed that the package is far too small. I therefore suspect that any claim, with the amount of bureaucracy within the European Union which seems to accompany anything appearing straightforward, will become a long-drawn-out uphill struggle for the growers. Hopefully the tenacity which they have shown in the past will prevail.

Cucumbers that wrongly got a bad press will feature in a Lea Valley Growers' Association festival in the grounds of Waltham Abbey.

As I have previously discovered, the Lea Valley Growers' Association have a resilient membership and in the face of what appears to be a major image crisis for their industry the fight back to regain their former market position has already begun. In the autumn of this centenary year they are planning to hold a Cucumber Festival within the grounds of Waltham Abbey where they will be aiming, amongst other things, to create a world cucumber record and I am confident that they will be successful in their endeavours.

Note. At the time of writing (August 2011) scientists now believe that the *E. coli* outbreak was in fact caused by the bean sprouts grown in Germany. However, with all the bad publicity and false information it will take the buying public some time to have their confidence restored, not just in the purchase of salad produce, but with future reports put out by scientists.

Cucumber Hoopla, a game devised to engage children and get them thinking about eating healthily when visiting the Waltham British Cucumber Festival.

Promoting the great British cucumber at the Waltham Abbey British Cucumber Festival. The event celebrated the importance of the Lea Valley which produces up to eighty percent of the UK's cucumbers.

CONCLUSION

While it would be naive to believe that everything between all the growers and all the supermarkets was the essence of sweetness and light, what I have discovered in carrying out the research for this book would suggest that the Lea Valley horticultural industry, although only twenty percent of its former size, has found and developed a formula for survival. At its height the Lea Valley had in the order of some 445 hectares of glass and approximately 550 growers and now with just 110 growers and 220 hectares of glass the horticultural industry can vastly exceed the quantity of produce grown by their predecessors. This has been achieved through a programme of glasshouse modernisation and the introduction of new technology into the growing areas.

One of the most important changes was the necessity for the industry to compete on price and quality and this has been achieved through major efficiencies by the core growers by vast improvements in economy of scale. It is therefore my view that to compete against foreign imports it is necessary for the growers not to get bogged down on lobbying government to have punitive tariffs placed on overseas produce (as we have seen in the past) but to form joint ventures and cooperatives with overseas suppliers. In this way economies of scale will be achieved and the outcome will put the Lea Valley Growers' Association on an equal footing with the large supermarkets because this will considerably enhance their ability to negotiate and, at the same time, reduce the controlling power of the large retailers. Once the growers have achieved this goal the grower, retailer and consumer will all benefit from a period of improved long-term price stability which will allow better control of company and household budgets.

In discussing, with both business and academic colleagues, how certain growers are achieving economies of scale by joint ventures and partnerships with nurseries abroad, the point is often raised that these growers could eventually pull out of the UK altogether and act as overseas suppliers. My response to this is to remind people that the UK consumer market is rapidly changing with consumers demanding more and more British produce and, with thoughts for our environment, a vast reduction in food miles. This in my view will encourage growers to remain in the UK and for these reasons it is hoped that government and local authorities will be more sympathetic to growers' expansion plans. For once, the authorities should recognise the worth of our horticultural industry and support it wholeheartedly by speeding up the planning process.

It should be remembered that the Lea Valley Growers' Association, in its hundred year history, has survived two World Wars, numerous storms, heat waves, freezes, floods, fuel shortages, including the Middle East oil crisis and on more than one occasion a global meltdown of the money markets. All these difficulties, while being financially challenging, have been overcome and the Lea Valley growers have shown much ingenuity and resilience. Let us all give our support to an industry that has helped feed Britain so that future generations can benefit from a supply of fresh food grown by an environmentally conscious industry.

REFERENCES

Allen, Mea (1970) *Tom's Weeds – the story of Rochfords and their house plants*. Faber & Faber, London.

Ashworth, William (1967) *An Economic History of England 1870 –1939*. Methuen.

Author unknown, "The Glasshouse Industry of the Lea Valley". The Lea Valley Growers' Association, (1968).

Author unknown (1957) "Eighty Acres of Glass – 75 years – a Joseph Rochford anniversary". *The Grower*, August 17th.

Author unknown (1932) "Father of the Glasshouse Industry". *The Market Grower & Salesman*, July 6th.

Author unknown (1961) *Golden Jubilee of the Lea Valley Growers' Association: October 1911–October 1961*. National Farmers Union, Hertfordshire.

Author unknown (2003) *Collaborative Research and Development: Waste Minimisation*. DTI Document.

Author unknown (2008) "Retailers must take lead in fair pricing". *Lea Valley Growers' Association's Newsletter,* Issue No: 395, December.

Barker, Kenneth (2006) *South from Barley, the story of the South family and Samuel South & Sons*. Self-published, London Colney.

Barnett, Sophie (2011) "Growers plea to planners: let us build glass". *Horticultural Week*, April 30th.

Cox, Peter (2010) *Spedan's Partnership, The story of John Lewis and Waitrose*. Labatie Books, Cambridge.

Currie, C R J (ed) (1995) *The Victorian History of the County of Middlesex – Hackney Parish Vol. 10*. University of London Press, London.

Dingemans, L A, former owner of L A Dingemans & Co., Ltd., Cheshunt, a private conversation and correspondence (August 2011).

Everett, David, Director, Anglo Aquarium Plant Company Ltd., Enfield, Middlesex, a private conversation, (February 2011).

Franklin, Andrew, Valley Grown Nurseries, a private conversation, (January 2009).

Giardina, Nick, Slough Nursery, Slough, Buckinghamshire, a private conversation, (February 2011).

Halladey, Ruth, Lea Valley Growers' Association, a private conversation, (June 2011).

Horsewood, Nicholas (2010) "Beggar Thy Neighbour: British imports during the inter-war years and the effect on the 1932 tariff". Department of Economics, University of Birmingham.

Jones, Caroline, Guy & Wright Limited, a private conversation and correspondence, (January 2009).

Leach, Peter, related to the famous Rochford family, a private conversation and correspondence (January 2011).

Lewis, Jim (1999) *London's Lea Valley, Britain's Best Kept Secret*. Phillimore & Co. Ltd., Chichester.

Lewis, Jim (2001) *London's Lea Valley, More Secrets Revealed*. Phillimore & Co. Ltd., Chichester.

Lewis, Jim (2004) *East Ham & West Ham Past*. Historical Publications Limited, London.

Lewis, Jim (2009) *Water and Waste: four hundred years of health improvements in the Lea Valley*. Libri Publishing, Oxford

Marchant, Andy (2003) "Grower of the Year Awards – Guy & Wright Ltd".

Martin, Roy (2007) *A History of Crews Hill and a step beyond*. Self-published, Enfield.

Middleton, C H (1941) *Your Garden in War-Time*. George Allen & Unwin Ltd., London.

Pelling, Henry (1976) *A History of British Trade Unionism*. Penguin Books, Harmondsworth.

Pignatelli, Yolanda, a senior executive at Glinwell, a private conversation, (February 2011).

Poulter, Sean (2011) "Major food alert as two Britons are diagnosed with fatal food poisoning bug traced to organic cucumbers". *Mail Online*, 28th May.

Renton, Alex (2011) "British farmers, facing ruin, pay cost of supermarket price wars". *The Observer*, July 3rd.

Rochford, Paul, a descendant of the famous Rochford family, a private conversation, (January 2011).

Rochford, Thomas, a descendant of the famous Rochford family, a private conversation and correspondence (August 2011).

Rooke, Peter (1997) "The Lea Valley Nursery Industry". *Hertfordshire's Past*, No.42, Hertfordshire Archaeological Council, Hertfordshire.

Rooke, Peter (1989) *Cheshunt at War 1939-45*". Self-published, Cheshunt.

Shaddick, Claire (2003) "Grower Power". *The Commercial Greenhouse Grower*, May issue.

Sheppherd, Mark, owner of L A Dingemans & Co., Ltd., nurseries, Cheshunt, a private conversation and correspondence (August 2011).

South, Christopher, a descendant of the famous South family, a private conversation and correspondence (January 2011).

South, Jim, (1977) "Nurserymen", unpublished article.

Stevenson R A (Tony), former secretary of the Lea Valley Growers' Association, a private conversation and correspondence, (March, 2011).

Stiles, Lee, Secretary of the Lea Valley Growers' Association, a private conversation and correspondence, (January 2011).

Taylor, Gary, Valley Grown Nurseries and chairman of the Lea Valley Growers' Association, a private conversation, (February 2011).

Thomas, Richard (2009) *The Explosions at the Royal Gunpowder Mills*. Published by the Royal Gunpowder Mills.

Walsh, Georgina (1976) "Where fortunes have gone with the wind". *Evening Standard*, Tuesday 6th January, 1976

Ward, Frank, Director, Hennock International Ltd, Nettleham, Lincolnshire, a private conversation, (January 2009).

Wilson, Alan, Technical Manager Agronomy Waitrose, a private conversation and correspondence (April 2011).

Minute Books/News Letters/Reports/Guide

Experimental and Research Station, Cheshunt, Hertfordshire "Annual Report (Thirty-fifth year) 1949", Nursery & Market Garden Industries' Development Society, Limited.

Experimental and Research Station, Cheshunt, Hertfordshire "Annual Report (Thirty-fifth year) 1953", Nursery & Market Garden Industries' Development Society, Limited.

Festival of Britain and Battersea Park Pleasure Gardens Guide, 1951.

Minute books of the Lea Valley Growers' Association from 1911–1939.

News Letters of the Lea Valley Growers' Association from 1948–1966.

Report by Reading Agricultural Consultants Ltd., in association with Gerry Hayman and Hennock Industries Ltd. "Viability of the Horticultural Glasshouse Industry in Epping Forest District; Prospects for the Future and Likely Scale of Development Over the Next 10 to 15 Years", Epping Forest District Council, (September 2003).

Oral History Project

Memories from Emilia Romanga and Sicily. Memories of Italian immigrants in the Lea Valley and London. The sound recordings and personal photographs have been deposited in the Camden Local Studies Archive, the Museum of Epping District Forest in Waltham Abbey and at Lowewood Museum, Borough of Broxbourne, (2006). Material from this oral history project will be permanently stored at the Emigration Archive Studies in Bedonia (Parma)

APPENDIX I
AN INTERESTING BUSINESS ARRANGEMENT!

As someone who has been involved in negotiations with contractors and other service providers where business was normally concluded with both parties agreeing to honour the terms and conditions of a legally binding contract, I was astonished to discover the type of arrangement that existed between Lea Valley growers and some of the large supermarkets which they were supplying with fruit and vegetables. While my business, in the consumer electronics industry, dealt with products and components that were not normally influenced too greatly by ambient temperatures, vagaries of the weather and shelf life, the trade of Lea Valley growers falls under a quite different category.

A typical display of fruit and vegetables at a Waitrose supermarket.

The fruit and vegetable section of the Waitrose store at Henley, 1965.

Intrigued by what I had learned I was fortunate in being able to correspond with a senior representative of Waitrose, part of the John Lewis Partnership, who was extremely helpful in answering a series of questions that I posed. Usually I have found such large organisations reluctant to discuss the type of business arrangements they have with their suppliers but Waitrose were very forthcoming and open and appeared to relish the opportunity to provide me with answers.

Q. How does the relationship between Waitrose and the grower develop and work?

A. Accepting that our strategy is to have close working relationships with our suppliers and growers, we have a number of initiatives which have been in place for many years to ensure each grower and supplier is aware of what's going on. For example, we hold an annual supplier technical conference, an individual supplier review and in most cases a growers' meeting. Waitrose has close relationships with several universities and we arrange technology transfer days which suppliers and growers may attend. I think you have seen clear evidence of the relationship working by the way we have come together for this email. In the case of [the Lea Valley grower in question] he has my phone number and will ring me whenever he wants to, for whatever reason. Often we are talking about how the crop is developing but sometimes it's a more serious trading issue which needs to be resolved. The key point is that because of our relationship with suppliers and growers, we hope that everyone feels comfortable to discuss any issue in a spirit of openness and honesty. This is an area often misunderstood by the media. I have been Technical Manager for Waitrose for many years and several of my team have been partners for over twenty years – myself; for thirty-seven. Such stability we think is essential in working with growers across the world who apart from being highly skilled, are also really nice people who understand the John Lewis Partnership.

Q. I presume that Waitrose would have to forward-plan in relation to the amount of produce it wanted, so would this lead to some form of contractual arrangement between yourself and the grower?

A. Each supplier regularly discusses the quantities required by the buyer. This is called a programme. It is the best guide we can give to what our requirement is likely to be over a season, but remember this is fruit and vegetables, and as I write to you it is 19th April and the outside temperature is 25°C. We have to cater for that and I would expect Lea Valley growers to be very busy today. The important thing to say in terms of predicting supply from growers is that we do not chop and change or make sudden decisions that leave people with vast quantities of stock that would be financially embarrassing for them. This would be bad business. Within the fruit and vegetable industry it is rare to find a contractual agreement of the type that you are alluding to. I think that you would be surprised to know how much is done on trust. It is a system that works when both parties have the type of relationship I have described.

Q. Could you give me some pointers of how you select your Lea Valley, or other, growers, do you visit the sites and once a grower is chosen do you monitor the supplier with follow-up visits?

A. Our suppliers, the people we trade with, could be growers, but more usually packers. We also have to consider importers. There is a key difference between all three. In some cases, the supplier is also the grower, packer and importer such as the [Lea Valley grower in question]. Therefore, the buyers will select the supplier who fits the assortment range we wish to buy. There is a move to much larger suppliers who have a vast range of products in different pack houses and different growers. Before any supplier is accepted as a supplier to Waitrose, they need to meet a fairly exhaustive list of requirements that refer to pack house standards and grower accreditation schemes. Above that the most important aspect of a supplier for Waitrose is their commitment and the availability of stock to meet our customer demands. We would visit any supplier before they start supplying and make routine follow-up visits. Many of our suppliers have been with us for over twenty years. Changing a supplier is a costly experience for us and also does not fit in with of our strategy which is to have close working relationships with both supplier and grower.

Q. What is your system of quality control?

A. The modern system of quality control is really called quality assurance. This means that the grower and supplier would have a number of systems in place to ensure that the specification we have agreed can be consistently adhered to. Fruit and vegetables are not exact tins of beans and therefore through our close working relationship with suppliers and growers, the characteristics of seasons and the challenges of weather patterns are accommodated for in the specification. All suppliers would have a quality control procedure which relates to the final packed product. Using our data we will check the quality upon

arrival at our depot, and monitor the quality into the branches. Customer complaints are taken very seriously. The success of a supplier's business is primarily based upon the quality standards being achieved. If quality cannot be achieved the stock will not be purchased.

I have chosen Waitrose to illustrate how the supplier retailer relationship works. However, it should be remembered that Waitrose, as part of the John Lewis Partnership, is a unique company in the way that it has been structured with each employee being part owner of the business. The formula ensures that staff take an active interest in the business and this is rewarded by the employee (partner) receiving a share of the annual profit in the form of a bonus payment.

When I was employed within the consumer electronics industry I had personal experience of dealing with members of the Partnership and can confirm the sentiment contained within the answers above, that they really are nice people to do business with.

In 1906 John Lewis, the founder of the business in Oxford Street that bears his name, bought the drapers business of the late Peter Jones, in Sloane Square, Chelsea from his sons, who appear not to have had an interest in running the firm they inherited from their father. By 1913, John seems to have lost interest in the Sloane Square shop and handed the chairmanship to his son, Spedan. Later in 1914 Spedan was given complete control of Sloane Square but had to relinquish his share in the Oxford Street store. The story goes that John and his son frequently did not see eye to eye on business matters and giving Spedan responsibility for the Peter Jones store was probably a test to see if he could cope.

Like many father and son relationships, it was probably the case of neither party wishing to accept or acknowledge the views and ideas of the other, especially in public. But when out of each other's earshot it is often the case that the adversaries, when speaking to others, express a warm mutual respect. It was not until after the death of John Lewis in June 1938 that Spedan began the task of introducing the partnership ideas, that he had begun at Peter Jones, into the rest of his late father's business. Here we see Spedan's feeling of respect for his late father showing through when he named the business the John Lewis Partnership.

In October 1937 the John Lewis Partnership branched out from its traditional drapery business by purchasing a chain of ten small grocery shops that were trading under the name of Waitrose. At the time it was thought sensible

Waitrose laboratory Mrs Vizoso makes microbiological anaylysis of food sample using laminar flow cabinet, 1988.

A Waitrose store pioneering the production and sale of organic produce, 1988.

not to change the company name and associate it with the John Lewis Partnership as some had thought the purchase was particularly foolhardy. The name Waitrose originates from the names of two of the three founder members of the company, Wallace Wait and Arthur Rose. The third member, David Taylor, left the company at an early stage in its development. When the business was subsumed into the John Lewis Partnership, all the one hundred and sixty-four employees were made partners and given the same terms and conditions as all other members of the organisation. From the joining over seventy years ago, Waitrose has developed into one of the United Kingdom's leading supermarkets, recognised for the quality of its products, no doubt influenced by the legacy of partnership, a formula that has worked well over the years, laid down by the extraordinary Spedan Lewis.

APPENDIX II
A LEA VALLEY HORTICULTURAL DYNASTY

There are many names that have served the Lea Valley horticultural industry over the years but there is one that stands out and across the generations and tends to feature more than any other and that name is Rochford.

In 1840 Michael Rochford, along with many other likeminded countrymen, crossed the Irish Sea and arrived in England. In that year alone, over 60,000 people left the old country in an effort to escape hunger and deprivation and seek a better life for themselves and their families elsewhere, particularly in countries such as England, America, Canada, New Zealand and Australia. Their timing was slightly ahead of the potato famine which is generally accepted to have reached its peak between the years 1845 to 1850. However, there had been many occasions in preceding years when the potato crop had failed, causing famine and hardship amongst a population that was already extremely poor.

Michael first shows up in England in the Chelsea 1841 census returns as a "gardener" living at 2 Symons Street

and his age is recorded as twenty years old. It is thought that Michael could have worked for Joseph Knight who, at about this time, had a nursery in Kings Road, Chelsea, but this is only speculation as records for this company no longer exist. However, there is a clue that might suggest that Michael was in the employ of Knight. Around the late 1840s Knight was joined by his nephew, Thomas Perry and they appear to have formed some sort of agency advertising to "send out Gardeners, Foresters, Bailiffs etc." to carry out work for their numerous patrons. In 1848 Michael married Sarah Mumford, a Chelsea girl, the daughter of a paper stainer (wallpaper maker) and it was during that year that Lord Nugent of Weedon near Aylesbury in Buckinghamshire required a gardener for his manor house "Lilies". Michael's marriage certificate records his connection with Lord Nugent, so it is likely that Lord Nugent could have obtained his plants from the nursery of Joseph Knight and would therefore have been aware of their advertisement to supply skilled workmen.

In November 1850 Lord Nugent, Michael's employer,

Michael Rochford who came from Ireland as a young man and founded a dynasty of nurserymen.

Sarah Mumford whom Michael Rochford married at Chelsea in 1848.

died and Michael and Sarah, now with a one-year-old son Thomas, found themselves back at Chelsea. According to Mea Allen, the author of *Tom's Weeds*, a book about Rochford's house plants, Michael, on returning to Chelsea, was "definitely" employed by Joseph Knight. The year after Michael's return to Chelsea was 1851 which saw the opening of the Great Exhibition in Joseph Paxton's uniquely designed Crystal Palace located in London's Hyde Park. It was also a happy year for Michael and Sarah with the birth of their second son John.

In the year 1852 we find Michael and his family in Helmsley, Yorkshire where he had secured a job on Lord Feversham's estate at Duncombe Park and it was here that their third child Mary was born. Michael's position was now of steward which meant he was in charge of all the outside gardening staff and had control of the estate's glasshouses and also responsibility for the formal and informal gardens. Although it is not known how Michael obtained this new position with Lord Feversham, it is likely that it may have had something to do with the advertising services of Joseph Knight and his nephew Thomas Perry.

While working at Duncombe Park it is thought that Michael came up with the idea of using putty only on the underside of the individual glass panes when glazing glasshouses. He had reasoned that applying a top line of putty to the glass was both unnecessary and wasteful. It also added to the weight of the roof on what was already a heavily over-burdened structure.

Some of the exotic fruits which were grown by Michael at Duncombe Park were pineapples, oranges, figs and grapes and the knowledge that he gained from their cultivation would no doubt prepare him for greater things in the future.

In 1856 Lord Feversham acquired Oak Hill, a large estate with a mansion in East Barnet, formerly known as Monkenfrith, then an area of woodland owned by St Albans Abbey. Michael was asked to take responsibility for the gardens and this would mean the whole family would have to move south. Since Michael and Sarah had been at Duncombe Park they had become rather productive and the infant members of the family had now risen to five. The Oak Hill estate had become famous for growing pineapples and grapes, two fruits that were to feature significantly in Michael's later life.

Michael and his family next turn up in Tottenham around the year 1857 and the following year he is recorded as living at 2 George Villas, Stamford Road, Page

Green and paying rates for house, garden and land. By the spring of that year Michael had erected two glasshouses and planted two varieties of grape, Black Hamburghs and Muscats. In 1860 Michael's family grew once more with the birth of twin boys; Michael and George.

By 1861, Michael was employing five men and a boy on his two-acre piece of land at Page Green and in the following year he is listed in the *London Directory* as a "Market gardener and florist". So in a little over twenty years since leaving his native Ireland, Michael had established himself as a businessman in his own right and had put down his marker in the Lea Valley. This would see the Rochfords blossom and grow into one of the most successful and respected names in the world of horticulture. Perhaps there is a lesson here for us all. Without dedication, sacrifice and sheer hard work it would be difficult to see how Michael could have achieved such a level of success and have placed his family on the path to fame and fortune in such a relatively short while.

Michael's arrival at Tottenham had almost coincided with the development of a new public water supply and a system for the disposal of sewage for Wood Green and Tottenham. Under the Public Health Act of 1848 Tottenham took the opportunity to establish a Local Board of Health to deal with an increasing level of unsanitary conditions. By the late 1840s the stench in the Page Green area must have been unbearable, particularly on hot summer days, as it has been estimated that around eight hundred dwellings were discharging their effluent waste directly into the Moselle Brook, a local waterway connected to the River Lea and close to Michael's land. Adjacent to Page Green is an open space which we now call Markfield Park and it was there that the Local Board of Health chose to build their sewage pumping station, filter beds, holding tanks and settlement tanks. By 1853 the Board claimed to have completed their scheme to supply clean drinking water to the built-up areas of Tottenham and Wood Green. However, due to the increased demand, mainly brought about by a rise in population as factories set up in the area, it was decided to extend the water works at Tottenham Hale. While all these improvements were taking place it would have been possible for Michael to have obtained water for his glasshouses and market garden from wells, as there were a number in the Page Green area.

Today, through the advances in media, we regularly learn of natural disasters such as hurricanes, flooding and severe storms as they happen around the world. Scientists have suggested that our insatiable consumption of energy, which relies heavily on the burning of fossil fuels, which in turn releases harmful CO2 emissions has contributed to the changes in our weather patterns. These relatively new manifestations have been blamed on a general rise in temperature, caused by these gas releases, and termed "global warming". However, today we hardly give a thought to the idea that similar extreme weather events occurred in London one hundred and fifty years ago, but occur they certainly did. In February 1860 Tottenham was struck by a hurricane of such force that large trees were uprooted and Michael's nursery suffered severe damage. His glasshouses were wrecked and the force of the wind caused shards of glass to rip through most of his plants. Fortunately his grape vines survived in reasonable shape. The overall damage to the nursery was estimated to be almost £1,000, a considerable amount of money at the time. Michael eventually built his business back up again as he no doubt had considerable incentive to do so.

In 1867 George, the tenth and last child was born. He was named after his brother, the twin of Michael, who had died in 1859 at the age of four.

Sixteen years after the hurricane wrecked Michael's nursery disaster struck again. In July 1876 a massive hail storm hit Tottenham which caused widespread damage to property across the region. Severe flooding occurred as drains became blocked and hailstones the size of large marbles penetrated roofs. Michael's glasshouses again suffered considerable damage and on this occasion his precious grape vines that were in fruit were cut to pieces. Helped by sons John and Joseph, Michael turned the disaster into an opportunity as they rebuilt the glasshouses with larger panes of glass to allow in more light and they also used less wood to make a lighter and improved roof structure.

Thomas Rochford (the first) with his mother and father.

Thomas Rochford I centre with his mother Sarah in the grounds of Turnford Hall.

Thomas Rochford I with his family at Turnford Hall.

The Rochford ancestral home, Turnford Hall, which in the 1970s sadly succumbed to the developer's hammer.

By 1871, Thomas, the eldest of the Rochford's children, had left his father's nursery at Page Green. Like many young men in the industry, when reaching a certain age (Thomas was twenty-one) he went on to gain further experience by working at the nursery of another grower. The nursery he chose was that of James Sweet who had a business in Church Road in the nearby village of Leyton. At the time there were many nurseries and market gardens in east and north London and it was these valuable pieces of green space that industry desired when it later expanded out of the capital. Helped by the growth of the railways, which allowed the workforce to travel relatively cheaply to follow the jobs, the nursery land also attracted the builders of low-cost housing. Soon villages like Tottenham, Walthamstow and Leyton, that once formed a ring around London, became boroughs of the Metropolis. These events, accompanied by the increasing amounts of industrial pollution, were the reasons which forced nurserymen to relocate further north up the Lea Valley where the air was cleaner and the water supply purer.

The year 1876 was a memorable one for Thomas as he married Mary Ann Agnes of Whitechapel, the daughter of an ivory cutter, and left his employer James Sweet of Leyton, setting up a nursery on his own account at Northumberland Park, Tottenham. Thomas had borrowed money from his mother to start the nursery, which must have been an almost instant success, as the loan was repaid after only one year. In 1877 Thomas and Mary's first child,

Thomas Samuel, was born, the second Thomas in the Rochford dynasty. Two years later George Michael came along and in 1882 Francis William arrived. At some time during this period, Thomas and Mary moved from their address at 26 Somerford Grove, Leyton, to 2 Cleveland Villas, Northumberland Park, Tottenham, to be closer to the nursery.

In 1882, two adjacent plots of land amounting to around eight acres were purchased at Turnford, Hertfordshire by Joseph, Michael's fourth son. Michael had originally agreed to buy the land so that John and Joseph could start their own nurseries but failing health had prevented him from doing this. Michael died in January 1883 at the age of sixty-four; a self made man, the proud founder of the Rochford Lea Valley horticultural dynasty.

Joseph sold one of the plots of land, about four acres that had once been part of the Turnford Hall estate to his brother Thomas. In 1887 Turnford Hall came onto the market and Thomas purchased it along with outbuildings and three acres of land for £1,200. By now Thomas and Mary's family had grown to four children so the house with its eight bedrooms would be ideal. In the coming years the number of children would increase to eight. The Rochford brothers, Thomas and Joseph, virtually made Turnford their own, expanding the land and the acreage of glass in their respective nurseries over the years many fold.

Thomas specialised in growing flowers, shrubs and palms while Joseph grew grapes and took on the relatively new branch of horticulture that was just emerging in England by growing tomatoes.

Turnford Hall logo used to advertise Rochford's nurseries at Turnford. This logo was printed on cartons of produce.

As the Turnford workforce grew, the Rochfords built terraces of houses for key workers and their families. Thomas began a Benefit Society by which employees earning over eight shillings a week contributed four old pence to the fund and those earning sixteen shillings paid six old pence. Senior members of the fund were paid twelve shillings per week when sick and junior members eight shillings. Any surpluses were divided amongst the members at Christmas time.

While it might appear to a twenty-first century observer that working for the Rochford's was an idyllic and secure occupation, in fact, by today's standards of employment, conditions were a little harsh. The working day normally ran from six in the morning until six at night with a one hour dinner break. There were no mid-morning or afternoon breaks for refreshment. Discipline was pretty strict and the consequences of this could even extend into the domestic life of employees. Through the entries recorded in the Staff Record Book we learn that a workman was dismissed "for using bad language at home". However, if you were punctual, worked hard and showed enthusiasm for your job you were likely to be rewarded with promotion and a long and secure career.

In a relatively short time the brothers had transformed the rather sleepy hamlet of Turnford into a place affectionately known by the locals as Rochfordville. Over the years other brothers and members of the Rochford family migrated to the upper Lea Valley, setting up their own nursery businesses and later they were followed by other generations of Rochfords as they carried on and expanded the nursery trade in the region. When we come to the setting up of the Lea Valley and District Growers' Association Limited in 1911, the names of J P Rochford and F Rochford are recorded in the minutes as two of the founding members.

Thomas Rochford III, third from right, between Princess Margaret and Anthony Armstrong Jones at Chelsea.

It is interesting to note how prolific the Rochfords were within the region of the Lea Valley below Cheshunt in the late nineteenth century. To illustrate this I have reproduced below the entries from the Tottenham, Enfield, Edmonton and Winchmore Hill Commercial Directory.

1893–4 Tottenham, Enfield, Edmonton and Winchmore Hill Commercial Directory
Rochford's Nursery, High Street Ponders End
Rochford, John, nurseryman and florist, Cedrus Lodge, Turkey Street, Enfield
Rochford, Michael, nurseryman, Arbour nursery, Brimsdown, Enfield
Rochford, Sarah (Mrs), florist, 2 George Villas, Stamford Road, South Tottenham

1894–5 Tottenham, Enfield, Edmonton and Winchmore Hill Commercial Directory
Rochford's Nursery, High Street Ponders End
Rochford, George, nurseryman, Page Green Nursery, South Tottenham
Rochford, John, nurseryman and florist, Cedrus Lodge, Turkey Street, W.C. and Green Street, Enfield
Rochford, Michael, nurseryman, Durants Arbour Ponders End

1898–9 Tottenham, Enfield, Edmonton and Winchmore Hill Commercial Directory
Rochford's Nursery, High Street Ponders End
Rochford, George, nurseryman, 51 Stamford Road, South Tottenham
Rochford, John, nurseryman and florist, Cedrus Lodge, Turkey Street, W.C.; Green Street, Enfield and Durant's Arbour Ponders End

1899–1900 Stamford Hill and Tottenham Commercial Directory
Rochford, George, nurseryman, 51 Stamford Road, South Tottenham

1900–1901 Stamford Hill and Tottenham Commercial Directory
No Rochfords listed.

The absence of the Rochfords from this early twentieth century directory suggests they had all left the area, probably because of the advances of industry and housing up the Lea Valley, and had moved to sites that were less polluted.

A testimonial presented to Thomas Rochford I in 1897 for setting up the Turnford Hall Nurseries Workmen's Institute.

The Queen Mother admires
a floral display designed by
Elizabeth Rochford, Paris 1959.

A champagne lunch (1960) celebrating Thomas III's golden year of
horticultural achievements.

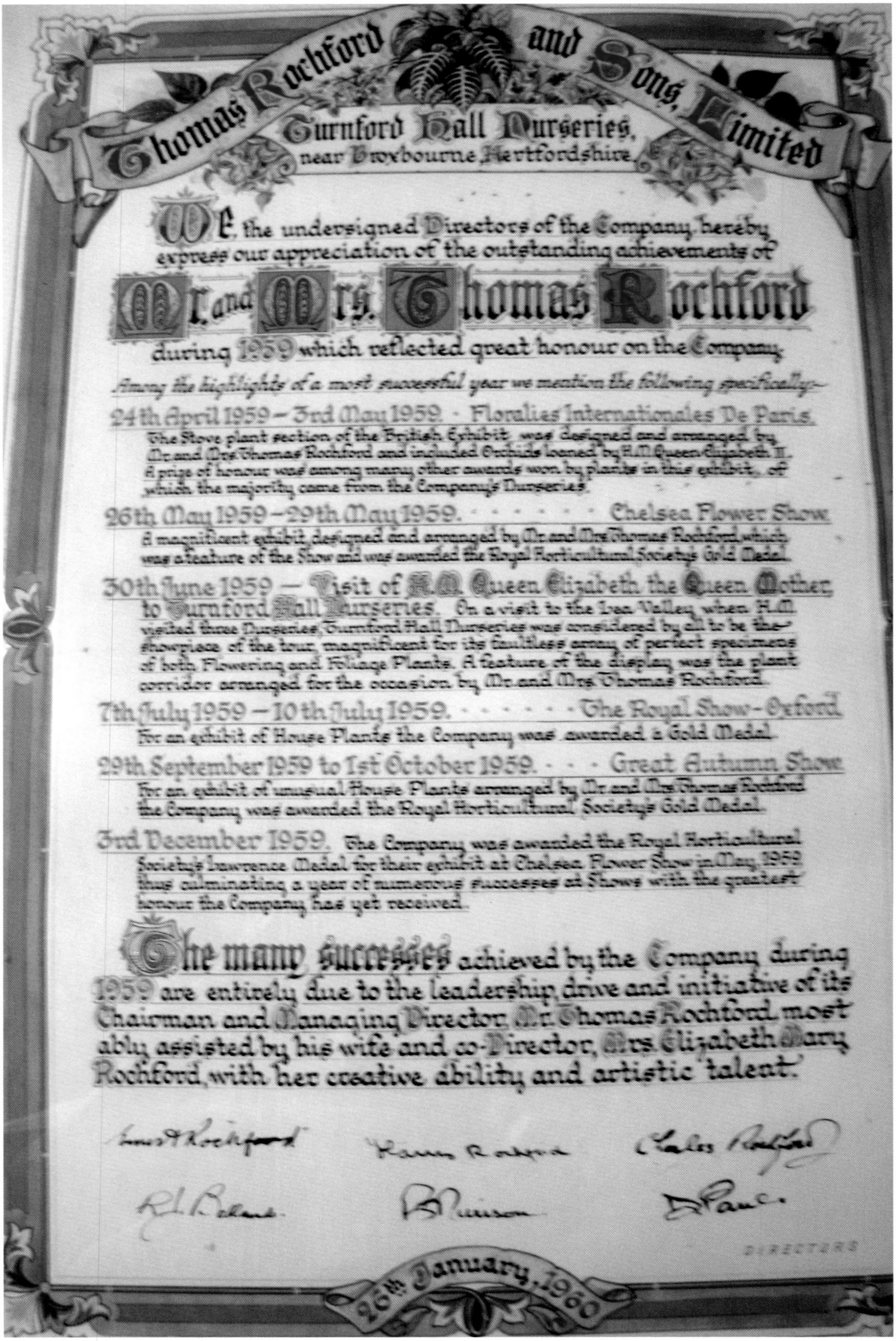

Thomas Rochford and Sons, Limited

Turnford Hall Nurseries, near Broxbourne Hertfordshire.

WE, the undersigned Directors of the Company, hereby express our appreciation of the outstanding achievements of

Mr. and Mrs. Thomas Rochford

during 1959 which reflected great honour on the Company.

Among the highlights of a most successful year we mention the following specifically:-

24th April 1959 – 3rd May 1959 · Floralies Internationales De Paris.
The Stove plant section of the British Exhibit, was designed and arranged by Mr and Mrs Thomas Rochford and included Orchids loaned by H.M. Queen Elizabeth II. A prize of honour was among many other awards won by plants in this exhibit, of which the majority came from the Company's Nurseries.

26th May 1959 – 29th May 1959. · · · · · · Chelsea Flower Show
A magnificent exhibit, designed and arranged by Mr and Mrs Thomas Rochford which was a feature of the Show and was awarded the Royal Horticultural Society's Gold Medal.

30th June 1959 — Visit of H.M. Queen Elizabeth the Queen Mother, to Turnford Hall Nurseries. On a visit to the Lea Valley when H.M. visited three Nurseries, Turnford Hall Nurseries was considered by all to be the showpiece of the tour, magnificent for its faultless array of perfect specimens of both Flowering and Foliage Plants. A feature of the display was the plant corridor arranged for the occasion by Mr and Mrs Thomas Rochford.

7th July 1959 – 10th July 1959. · · · · · · · The Royal Show - Oxford.
For an exhibit of House Plants the Company was awarded a Gold Medal.

29th September 1959 to 1st October 1959. · · · Great Autumn Show
For an exhibit of unusual House Plants arranged by Mr and Mrs Thomas Rochford the Company was awarded the Royal Horticultural Society's Gold Medal.

3rd December 1959. The Company was awarded the Royal Horticultural Society's Lawrence Medal for their exhibit at Chelsea Flower Show in May, 1959 thus culminating a year of numerous successes at Shows with the greatest honour the Company has yet received.

The many successes achieved by the Company during 1959 are entirely due to the leadership, drive and initiative of its Chairman and Managing Director, Mr. Thomas Rochford, most ably assisted by his wife and co-Director, Mrs Elizabeth Mary Rochford, with her creative ability and artistic talent.

DIRECTORS

26th January, 1960

A testimonial presented to Thomas and Elizabeth Rochford III for their many horticultural achievements in 1959.

Chelsea Pensioners on a visit to
Rochford's nurseries, Turnford c1970.

A Rochford lorry that not only delivered nursery products but also advertised their house plants boldly.

APPENDIX III
A CHANCE ENCOUNTER!

While attending a book-signing event held at Stratford Old Town Hall earlier this year I was asked by a member of the public, who had noticed the Lea Valley series titles of my books, if I knew anything about the development of the fertiliser Maxicrop. I immediately confessed my ignorance of the product. However, when researching archive material for this book I discovered that the name appeared regularly in advertisements within the News Letters of the Lea Valley Growers' Association.

I was told the story of Reginald Frank Milton, the inventor of what became known as Maxicrop, by John Buekett, a maternal relative of the man. Milton was born in West Ham in 1906 and in the early 1930s obtained a BSc in Chemistry after studying at Sir John Cass College, now part of London Metropolitan University. Later in the 1930s Milton is said to have worked with Dr Edgar Obermer, a pioneer in the use of the analysis of body fluids to aid medical treatment.

By the outbreak of the Second World War Milton had set up his own practice and was in business as a biochemist and analytical chemist with an address in Paddington. As the War progressed Milton found he was not able to obtain sufficient work and was given the choice of joining the Army or working at the Chemical Warfare Establishment at Porton Down, Wiltshire. He opted for the latter and was given the assignment of investigating alginates, extracted from seaweed, as a substitute for hemp. Hemp was traditionally imported from India and the material was in great demand during the war for making such things as camouflage netting. During Milton's work some liquor extracted from seaweed was discharged onto the ground outside his laboratory and he noticed that the weeds grew with unusual vigour.

In 1952 Reginald Frank Milton was granted patent No. 664989 for "Improvements in or relating to Horticulture and Agriculture Fertilisers" which covered the production of liquid fertiliser from seaweed by heating under pressure with dilute alkali carbonate. The patent was jointly in the name of Plant Productivity Limited and Milton. The name Maxicrop was conferred on the product which subsequently became available for commercial use in the early 1950s.

Maxicrop a seaweed-based fertiliser that was first discovered by accident.

APPENDIX IV
A COMPLEMENTARY GATHERING

Throughout Britain it will be recognised that when an industry becomes established in a particular area of the country, component and service suppliers to that industry begin to set up in close proximity and sometimes new suppliers and complementary companies are "spun off" from the grouping. For example the post-war automobile industry with many of its supply chain companies became established around the Birmingham area. And more locally the electronics industry that can trace its historic roots to Ponders End, Enfield at the beginning of the twentieth century spawned a cluster of associated companies in Brimsdown, Enfield and Tottenham.

One of the flower pot drying sheds of Messrs South, White Hart Lane, Tottenham. Thousands of these pots were supplied to the Lea Valley horticultural industry.

was a supplier of hundreds of thousands of clay flower pots to the Lea Valley nursery industry, are only distant memories of those of a certain age in the region. In turn these two Tottenham companies succumbed to the pressures of changing demand and falling business, the sites being sold to accommodate the next generation of light industry and warehousing.

A workman, believed to be a member of the South family, holds contrasting size flower pots.

As the horticultural industry became established in the upper Lea Valley a whole plethora of supply chain and service industries grew up close by to seize a business opportunity. There were companies who specialised in supplying manures and fertilizers, produce-handling equipment, glasshouse sterilising and cleaning services, complete glasshouses, flower pots and much more. Most of these companies, like their counterparts across the country, have disappeared as the core industry (in the case of the Lea Valley, the nursery businesses) began to contract. Names such as Duncan Tucker, a manufacturer of glasshouses in Lawrence Road, Tottenham and Samuel South, of White Hart Lane, Tottenham who

Samuel South (the Tottenham flower pot manufacturer) sitting on the inside, second row from back, during a visit by florists to Baltimore, America, March 1911.

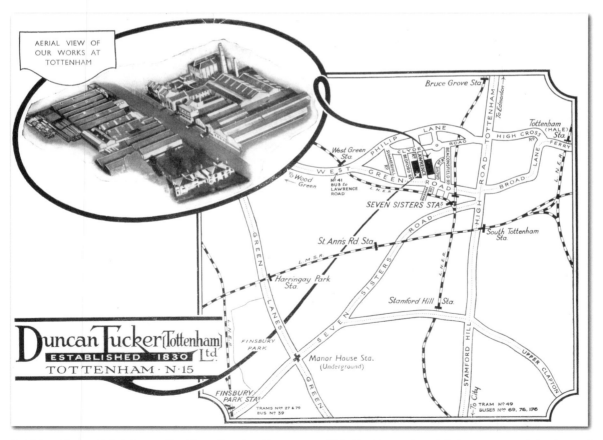

Aerial view of Duncan Tucker's Lawrence Road factory, Tottenham. The company, established in 1830, manufactured glasshouses; many supplied to the Lea Valley horticultural industry. The Duncan Tucker factory was replaced in the post-war period by a Thorn Lighting plant, which stopped production in the 1980s.

APPENDIX V
THE ATTRACTION OF GROWERS

Crews Hill, Enfield takes its name from William Crew, a local gamekeeper and rogue who, in the eighteenth century, once owned a house and barn in the area. According to the author Roy Martin, a few nurseries began to become established around the time of the First World War. It is said that the number of these nurseries and smallholdings increased when servicemen returned and bought land in the area with their service gratuities.

Today the area around Crews Hill attracts visitors from far and wide as it has become a local hub for garden centres that can supply anything from a ball of twine to a range of exotic plants. The established or aspiring gardener can acquire a range of paraphernalia for the enhancement or the design of a new out-of-this-world garden and, if the desire should take them, the plants, animals and equipment to fashion a pond, or perhaps a lake! And if carnivorous plants are your thing, these can be obtained too.

Relatively little growing takes place at Crews Hill today although there is some preparation and production of bedding plant packs for some of the superstore type of garden centres. With the increasing amount of gardening magazines and television programmes that currently flood the market and feed the consumer's seemingly insatiable appetite for new ideas, Crews Hill gardening centre complex looks set to weather the present financial downturn.

One of the many establishments at Crews Hill, Enfield that just about supply every conceivable product and shrub to beautify the garden.

Phoenix Rose garden centre, Crews Hill, Enfield.

Plants on display at the Phoenix Rose garden centre, Crews Hill, Enfield.

The Enfield Garden Centre, Crews Hill, Enfield.